Our Land Too

TONY
DUNBAR

OUR LAND TOO

With an Introduction by
ROBERT COLES

VINTAGE BOOKS

A Division of Random House
New York

Originally published by Pantheon Books in 1971.

ISBN: 0-394-71735-X
Library of Congress Catalog Card Number: 72-135040

Manufactured in the United States of America

First Vintage Books Edition, April 1972

TO RESISTERS
everywhere in this world,
and in memory of a warm person,
JAN BECKHARDT

Introduction

I have no wish in this introduction to come forth with paragraphs of uncritical praise, seasoned with a few efforts at synopsis. Mr. Dunbar is a serious young man, and he has done a first-rate job of describing what life is like in rural Mississippi and Appalachia, among other places in this rich and powerful nation. Since he is a good writer, as well as a thoughtful and careful observer, the reader needs no interpretation, no preliminary sermon that urges, prompts, reminds, explains, and insists. The pages ahead will soon enough compel their own attention, and for that I can only thank the author, as I believe others will want to do after they have finished this book. I do, however, want to say something about *Our Land Too*; I want to say something about the tradition to which the book belongs, and if the author will forgive me, I want to say something about his youth, his utter lack of credentials, his failure to "prepare" himself with "training" for the ever-so-complicated business of "research" he has so prematurely undertaken.

In the summer of 1936 a young man in his twenties left

New York City for Alabama because he wanted to learn how sharecroppers and tenant farmers lived. With him went a photographer (they were planning to do an article for a national magazine), and no doubt it is fair to say that the two men took with them the following "research materials": some pieces of paper, a pencil or two, a fountain pen, a camera. The men had not prepared a "proposal" for foundations, nor had they spent time writing up a "design" for their "investigation" or a statement of the "methodology" they intended to pursue. Upon their return they proclaimed no "results," no "findings" or "conclusions." They said they were troubled, were confused, were torn by a whole range of conflicting feelings. And indeed, as one goes through their long book one feels on every page a certain rambling quality, a strain of indecisiveness, a tone of perplexity. And one looks in vain for "strategies" or "techniques," for a theory about this or a formulation about that. Instead, James Agee and Walker Evans give us a book with the unlikely and incurably "romantic" title *Let Us Now Praise Famous Men*; give us a book that emphasizes life's ambiguities and ironies; give us a book that seems almost dedicated to emotions like wonder, awe, admiration —in contrast, that is, to brainy self-assurance, messianic zeal, political self-righteousness or academic snobbery.

Tony Dunbar is also in his twenties, his very early twenties. Unlike James Agee he doesn't even have a college degree. In fact, the work, the *living* it was, that prompted the writing of this book was done by what we call a "dropout." After a year or two of college Mr. Dunbar felt the need to leave, to travel, to go see, to go hear, to pay attention not to himself and his hangups and his "problems" and his sense of "alienation" and his present "goals" or his future "plans"—but rather to a portion of the larger world about him. So, he set out and traveled and eventually arrived in the Mississippi Delta.

There he tried to learn from men and women and children, who became his teachers. There he struggled, as James Agee did, as young George Orwell did, to comprehend not "problems" or "disadvantages" or "deprivations," but *lives*—yes, lives heavily burdened and threatened and terribly hurt, but lives also full of stubborn, unyielding determination and lives marked by moments of humor and generosity and kindness. There he also struggled to get the facts. How much money do these particular American citizens make? What kind of work do they find, if they can find any? Precisely how do they live—which means in what buildings and with what furniture or food or clothes? What do they see ahead for themselves? Do they have much hope? Do they lack spirit and vitality? Do they feel as sorry for themselves as some of us are wont to feel for them—during those occasional moments that interrupt our busy, important lives?

The result of Mr. Dunbar's failures as a college student was a thoroughly successful monograph ("The Will to Survive") published by the Southern Regional Council, a group of white and black southerners who are also dropouts of sorts, dropouts from the racism and bigotry and meanness and exploitation that have characterized that lovely, hate-filled, much scapegoated region whose writers (William Faulkner, Eudora Welty, Flannery O'Connor, Walker Percy) know a thing or two about how men and women manage to survive against high odds indeed—and I refer not only to hurdles like poverty and the legacy of slavery, but the peculiar loneliness and inwardness, the psychological jeopardy it is, a "soul" can sometimes experience out in those isolated and apparently Godforsaken villages and hamlets of the "black belt" or in thriving but uneasy cities like Memphis or Atlanta or New Orleans. The title of Mr. Dunbar's monograph and the title of his book tell us how he is inclined to look at those who are hard-pressed and unquestionably in certain respects doomed. They suffer, but they persist. They need our "help," but they demonstrate certain qualities that by no means are universally found among well-to-do intellectuals: a lack of nervous self-consciousness, a certain kind of tact and grace, a faith in God that will not be deterred, a wry and detached "world-view," not unlike an existential philosopher's or a Christian theologian's. Put differently, we are to learn in this book what people *have* as well as need. Particularly in the section that takes up the world of Appalachia we must contend with (almost) the author's unwillingness to make us the comfortable philanthropists, yet again asked to take up a few more liberal causes, write out an additional check or two, maybe sign another petition.

Up those hollows and creeks live people who are proud, who want no part of us, really—who want only work and money. It *is* their land; their ancestors came to this country, as did the slaves, a long, long time ago, and they every day give to the American land all the passion and concern they can muster. They work the land for food. Some of them still wrest coal from the land. They walk the land, hunt the animals who also live off the land, catch the fish that fill up the many rivers and lakes that cover the land. They know the land's needs; know its virtues and its limitations. They also know the pain that goes with seeing kin leave the land for the city, for distant and strange and crowded places that offer a degree of sanctuary to the hungry and jobless, but also "a long sleepless night," as I once heard a mountaineer from Kentucky describe his two years in Chicago. Nor are states like Mississippi or Alabama only the property of their foul-mouthed politicians or lawless sheriffs or violence-prone State Police. The poor of those states, regardless of race, also love the land; love the pinewoods; love the promising sunrises and flaming sunsets; love the wideness of the countryside, the elbowroom, the sounds of chickens or pigs, the sight of birds and bushes and wild flowers, the feel of feet touching pine needles or grass, the feel of a worm in the hand or of a turtle or a toad.

We who live in cities and call ourselves "educated" and buy books like this one tend to overlook the attachment, even reverence a sharecropper can feel for the earth he doesn't own and often fails to subdue. Over and over again we demand justice for the poor, but are not so willing to discover what form that justice would take if the poor had *their* way. And how can we know? We have our own lives, tied as they are to cities and professions and universities and particular newspapers or magazines. When we travel it is not ordinarily to eastern Kentucky's hollows or Mississippi's back roads and dirt paths and small, dusty towns that can be entered and left within seconds when driving one of today's cars. We know statistics, and our hearts are no doubt moved when a story or an article reaches us, or when a moment of historical change comes upon us; but for the most part our sympathies can only be vague and inactive and worst of all abstract—*for* "blacks" or *against* "segregationists."

Nor do some social scientists help us. They give us more abstractions. help us feel better informed, more in command of numbers, percentages, and a host of "explanations," often phrased in language guaranteed to stop the heart and dampen the spirit and clutter the mind. And the irony of it is that for all the "studies" and "projects" done in twentieth century America only certain things get investigated—which is to say we are victims of our own particular intellectual prejudices. If we set out to "expose poverty," measure the "cultural deficits" of people, show how "retarded" they are and how saturated with apathy and ignorance and despair—then we find what we are looking for, and in the bargain spend millions of dollars on the incredible refinements of surveys and "controlled experiments" and "in-depth" analyses. Meanwhile we have as fellow citizens the mountaineers and sharecroppers and former tenant farmers Tony Dunbar has visited and lived with and tried to bring before us. Have our many methodical investigators, our thousands of social scientists, managed to tell us more about Alabama's sharecroppers than James Agee did, or more about Mississippi and Appalachia than Tony Dunbar offers in this book?

Our Land Too is the work of a keen social observer, a fine essayist—and a young social observer or a young essayist will not usually find such interests and capacities sanctioned by our universities as "academic fields" in which students can "concentrate" or "major." I hope this book is read by great numbers of young Americans who are tired of the pomposities and banalities that flourish in many of those universities. I hope many, many young Americans, yet to die in spirit, will be able to see what achievements were possible for one of their age and their inexperience.

A century ago one would talk not of the *motivations* a "researcher" had, or the *data* he accumulated, but of the *sensibility* in a young man, and what came of that sensibility when he sat down to write. Because Mr. Dunbar used his eyes and ears and head and paid attention to his heart, he was able to record faithfully two human scenes, as it were. And because he has done so, we the educated have a chance to learn what others (the uneducated) have to say, and to teach.

If I had more confidence that any number of changes are soon forthcoming in our universities and our public life, I would say that this book will inspire many colleges and universities to change their notion of what a "course" is, how students learn, what young and sensitive men and women might *do* during those four years they spend as "students" in places called "institutions of higher learning." But I fear this book will budge certain people not an inch: bureaucrats of all sorts, parochial experts, those in medicine and law and the universities and government who can always find sanctuary in the infinite recesses that professional double talk always provides. If some readers find that this book's author has done enough, even more than enough in praise of famous men James Agee and Walker Evans once sang of and hailed and grieved for and rejoiced in, then I fear others will rather quickly recognize *Our Land Too* for the threat it presents not just to entrenched political and economic interests, but to many of us who are educated to the nth degree—which often enough comes to mean stiff and haughty and self-satisfied, if not fatally compromised.

ROBERT COLES

Foreword

A nation which has existed only a few hundred years may not be expected to have too much in the way of foundations. We in America, however, have built with amazing speed, and whatever stages in the process of development we have skipped in fact we have created in our imagination. A belief very dear to us is that there was once a time when a harmonious relationship was established between men and the work which they did, that honest enterprise, untainted by exploitation, was the keystone of American growth. We like to think that the great energy which set this country on its way was provided by men whose toil was spurred on by a vision of a bountiful future for all. We have attributed to our ancestors a commonness of purpose and a simplicity of life they did not have.

Our nation today has become a very sour place to live. There is very little to promise peace, security, or satisfaction to any of us. It is our basic feeling that in some way we have deviated from the promise of America more clearly seen by our forebears. To get to the source of the problem, we search about in our society to try and find the culprits who are causing all of this trouble.

It would be better if we took an honest look at some places where the reflection of the past is still clear; where we can get a more true idea of how it was that this country was built. America has not really changed much over the years in its conduct toward land and people. Where that conduct leads us can be seen in the Delta of Mississippi and in the mountains of East Kentucky.

No two regions have figured more prominently in the growth of America than the cotton lands of the South and the coal belt of the Appalachian Mountains. The one gave us a great agricultural empire, and the other gave us the power to run our machines and the raw material to build our cities. If ever this country laid foundations, they must be found in these areas. If anywhere we can hope to find a past real enough to learn from and a clear representation of attitudes that were and are central to the American system, it is in the mountains and the Deep South.

In rural America, the greatest concentration of poor blacks is in the Deep South; the greatest concentration of poor whites is in the southern Appalachians. Both areas have had their economies geared to one central output, one main source of work. Both have experienced the shift from plentiful jobs to unemployment created by automation. Both areas lack any modern industry and are extremely vulnerable to any industry which thrives on the economic castaway—the displaced tenant farmer or the out-of-work coal miner—who can be got to work dirt-cheap.

Both areas have experienced major social upheavals. The United Mine Workers' sweep of the mountains under John L. Lewis was the greatest union spectacle in our history. Mississippi felt the impact of the civil rights movement probably more than did any other Dixie state. Both areas are still very much in turmoil.

Mississippi and Appalachia are this country's best-known poverty areas. As real places—American as Texas and Florida, as the home of real people—not creatures to be experimented with but men to be dealt with, they have been largely forgotten by outside Americans because they have been mentioned so often. They have been neglected, to our continuing loss, as places where our system's attitudes toward people, the land and its resources, and the future can be evaluated. The War on Poverty struck with unmatched fanfare in these areas. Yet only feeble efforts have been made to change things, and little has been learned here.

It is unlikely that any one book can give a sense of the great stretch of history encompassed by the mountains and the Delta. This work tries only to show where that history has left the men and women who today have inherited these regions. The author lays no claim to being entirely objective. Though nearly all the statements made on tape for the section on Kentucky were included, only about a quarter of the dialogue, taken from about two-thirds of the interviews, were included in "The Will to Survive."

Throughout this book are the thoughts, expounded by several persons, that poor people must be viewed as men and women and as neighbors, not as statistics; that the solutions to their problems lie less in welfare doles than in radical alterations of the economics governing poor communities; that the people who have a problem are most likely to have the clearest insight as to how to solve it, and that the problems of the poor in Mississippi and Kentucky are shared, though not yet felt, by each of us across this land.

Contents

Author's Note

The two sections of this book, "The Will to Survive" and "Once The Promised Land," were prepared respectively in the fall of 1968 and during all of 1969. The first is an account of conditions in the Mississippi Delta as reported by some one hundred families who live there and tenant-farm on plantations. The second is an attempt to describe the people and the problems of the Kentucky mountains as viewed by this writer and by a retired coal miner, resident of one of the state's poorest counties.

Part I
THE WILL TO SURVIVE

❨ Well, you know what I figure about it, if I treat you right, you treat me right. That's the way I feel. A man is a man regardless to the size. You're a man just like I is, only thing is you're white and I'm dark, but we're still men. I ain't gonna come back here and curse you just like you're an old dog. You know I just don't feel that's right in my book. If I curse you, why you can curse me. Kick me, hit me, treat me like a dog—why that ain't right. I've heard fellers say, Now you take that one-armed son of a bitch and knock him in the head. I say, No, ain't nobody gonna knock me.

Quit talkin' about my luck. You can have it son. I cut my arm off in a truck side-swipe, and they couldn't help me, but still, anything you ask me to do, I'm willin' to do it, see.

A black tenant farmer, beaten and shot to death in the spring of 1970 after an incident outside a "white" nightspot in Louise, Mississippi. His body was later dragged from the Sunflower River.

The Louise-Midnight area, like all the Delta, is plantation country. About half of the white men in Louise own, manage, or are agents on plantations. The others are small farmers, factory workers in Belzoni (fifteen miles to the north), or work at such jobs as service station attendants and mechanics. Almost all the black families are tenant farmers on plantations, though some are sharecroppers and small farm owners. Louise and Midnight are towns that were built originally for the convenience of planters who preferred to shop, and to have their tenants shop, at stores nearby that they themselves owned. The borders of the towns are also the borders of plantations. When U.S. 49, running north through Louise to Belzoni and south to Yazoo City, was paved in the late 1940s, they were, as it is said, put on the map.

Louise is a row of about fifteen grocery, clothing, and auto parts stores along the highway, a post office, a plantation company headquarters, a doctor's office, a cafe, a dairy bar, three gas stations, a cotton gin, and a huge bean elevator. Behind the shops on one side of the highway is a paved street where the white townsfolk live. Behind the elevator

3

on the other side is a network of dirt roads cut by the Illinois Central Railroad, where the black families live. Regardless of the official town estimate of 481 population, Louise looks to have about three hundred people within its town limits.

Midnight is barely a town at all; it is not incorporated. It has two stores, one gas station, and two company cotton gins. The homes of the tenant farmers come right up to the highway. The town is so small that generally it will not be mentioned in this report. The Louise community can be understood to include Midnight and the surrounding area, most of which is divided into several large plantations. The large plantations have from five to twenty regularly employed tenants. There are several smaller plantations with fewer than five tenant families, and there are many individually operated farms.

I lived in the homes of poor black families in the country between Louise and Midnight for seven weeks during September, October, and November of 1968. With the help of some very courageous citizens of those towns and the receptiveness of the black community as a whole, tape recordings were made of forty-five-minute-long interviews with ninety-seven poor families in Louise and on surrounding plantations and with three community leaders. During the course of the project, only two families refused to be interviewed. The ninety-seven families whose interviews were taped have a total membership of 690 people, of whom 500 are children. The average family size is 7.1 persons. Average family income is $1,538 a year; per capita income of the 690 people is $216. The chief suppliers of income are the plantation, Social Security, and welfare.

The number of families whose statements were recorded represent approximately one-fifth of those in the black community in the Louise area, and, in fact, approximately one out of every thirty-seven families, white and black, in the county. Though the study was concerned only in an incidental way with the whole of Humphreys County, the people covered by the interviews account for one out of every twenty-nine in the total population of the county. (Each interview in the text is designated by a ◖.)

Without exception, the black people of Louise are poor, neglected, and deprived of everything that makes life pleasant, comfortable, or simple. This report is a description of the things that make the lives of the poor in the Delta not so much liveable as possible, and why existence is becoming more difficult in each succeeding year.

The title, "The Will to Survive," was chosen, rather than one relating directly to food problems, because it is hard to say which is worse—a man's hunger, or, say, the fact that he almost froze to death in the winter because his house was unsound and unheated. Poverty does not produce situations where a family has some major problems and some minor ones. All problems are major, and all needs are filled only with great difficulty. For the poor man, however, survival implies, above all else, obtaining food, and the poorer he is, the more he is involved in trying to provide food for his family. It is for him a constant struggle and a constant searching.

❢ I think it's terrible here. Mississippi is real terrible. I think the plantation is terrible, too, because all the people have to depend on is the work on the plantation, and most of the people living on the plantation don't ever get a chance to work.

I The Plantation

October is the first cold month in the Mississippi Delta. In the very early morning hours, a mist rises from each dew-and-frost-covered plant in the long straight rows of cotton. It drifts up out of the ditches, out of the creeks, out of the swamps. The first sunlight, streaking through the fringe of trees that mark the border between one man's land and another's or between what has been cultivated and what (with all the promise of a country farmed for over 150 years and still holding out more) has yet to be cleared, brings the mist alive, making the asphalt seem to shimmer and disappear in front of a driver, obscuring the dirt roads that branch out occasionally due east and due west, and turning into dark shadows the stumps and trees that grow, five feet deep in water and mud, in the stillness of the swamps.

As the sun rises, the mist thins away and the flat fertile land of the Delta reveals itself. From Memphis, Tennessee, to Yazoo City, Mississippi, a distance of some 175 miles, there is barely a rise in the plain except for the levees that wind beside the rivers flowing toward the Mississippi. Across those miles of endless field—cotton and soybean—trees serve as landmarks ("Go on down the gravel and turn down the road headin' toward that tree yonder"), and towns three miles distant can be located by their water towers or bean elevators. By nine o'clock tractors, mechanical cotton pickers, and bean combines are in the field. By ten o'clock it is hot. The land dries out. Long billowing clouds of dust follow the old automobiles and pickup trucks as they rumble along the dirt roads.

All day long the heat builds up. The sun shines pale yellow in the sky. Trailers full of cotton and bean trucks take over the blacktops, on the one side, into the fields, and on the other toward the gins and weighing stations where the drivers will see to the unloading of their vans and drink a bottle of Coke.

A haze of heat, dust, crop spray, and smoke comes up in the late afternoon. It coats the faces and arms of the men in the fields and fouls their machines. The sun begins to set near six o'clock. Even after it is gone, wide orange and red streaks of light hang against the horizon like clouds of compressed heat left behind. They are still there when, an hour later, the men head home because it has turned too dark and cold to work. Only rarely, when there is a great rush to get in the crop, will men be kept at work long after dark; then, late at night, the headlamps of their combines can be seen moving slowly up and down the fields, through the chilly fog, while only the faraway lights of town remain lit.

Five years ago everybody who needed to and anyone who wanted to—men, women, and children too young for school —would have been working in these fields in October, picking cotton at $2.50 per 100 pounds. Some of the children would have put down their sacks to catch the school bus; most would have kept to their work. They would have worked through the day, eating for lunch and supper sandwiches that they had stuffed in their pockets. Many of the women would have their babies with them. Each time a bag was filled, it would be dragged to the storage shed to be weighed and that weight logged beside the picker's name. The people would stay in the fields until well after dark, when at the signal of the agent all of the hands would stand up, straighten out their backs, and stand in line until each's name was called, the pounds each had picked totaled, and the wage, minus the rental fee for the bag, figured and paid out. The trucks would come and take them home.

❰ *How many men work this plantation now?*
They got about six of 'em, steady drivers.
Just as a guess, how many families would have been working here ten years ago?
About thirty of 'em.
Men, women, and children?
Everybody, yes sir. Them that wasn't big enough was out there. They was out there makin' a day.

❰ There used to be a whole lot more people on the plantations than there are now. The machines started long back in '50. I believe it started really back in '53, '54. Then every year they begin to get more and more, more and more, and that begin to cut people down out of pickin', you know. In other words, before that they were pickin' all the crop. Then after machines got in, they started pickin' ends, see. And so now, the biggest of 'em not pickin' none.

Almost all of the land surrounding Louise is divided into plantations. The smallest ones are only a few hundred acres; the largest are many square miles. Plantation land is farmed in two ways: by tenant farmers or by sharecroppers, all of whom are black. A tenant farmer (or what could better be called a tenant family) lives on the plantation in a house provided by the planter. In exchange for this, he is on call day or night, year round, to do any work that the planter requires, and he is paid for his work. Sharecropping, which has been considered virtually extinct for fifteen years, still persists in scattered instances around Louise. A sharecropper is given a piece of land, usually less than twenty acres, to farm. At harvest, he splits his crop between himself and the planter. Though the ratio between what the planter collects and what the cropper is left with is generally 60–40, they divide the crop evenly in Louise. To make any cash income at all, a sharecropper must double as a tenant farmer.

(This is the way it is on the plantation. You borrow money during the winter to help take care of your family. So when you start work, you're gonna work—now a tractor driver don't make but about six to eight dollars a day, and he gotta pay this man half of this money out of his wages, for what he borrowed back in the winter. And after this, well it's gonna start rainin' and things, well he got to go back and borrow some more money. Well he's just sold there. And he just pay him anything he wants to pay him—just give him anything—because he's there. He owes the man. He can't do nothin'. He got to take what he gets. Or either run off . . . . Yeah, they'll starve you off. I once heard that they say if you can't beat 'em, starve 'em to death.

A plantation, in the real sense, is an authoritarian world, ruled by a planter, where families earn with their sweat and labor the privilege of staying alive. The plantation system easily absorbed the shift from slavery to paid labor. Workers were simply paid too little money to live and went immediately in debt to the planter. The numerous ways of putting a tenant in debt were the planter's tools in exercising his authority. Tenants exhausted their cash at company stores and began to buy on credit. At times, the exchange was simplified by paying labor in scrip for use at company-owned stores. When he needed medical care, a tenant would go see his boss, who would provide a doctor and deduct the expense from the wage. When he needed a loan to provide for his family in the winter, the tenant would go to the planter. With the advent of electricity, the planter paid tenants' light bills and reduced by that much their paychecks.

The planter remained the boss in his land. He settled all disputes between his tenants in his own way. The horrible stories of the treatment of black tenant farmers by the white overseer, now called an agent, are probably almost all true. No sheriff would arrest a tenant without the permission of the planter, and it was often withheld for some planters preferred to exact their own punishments. No sheriff would refuse to arrest a man fingered by the planter. It is quite likely that some Mississippi law enforcement officers never saw more of many plantations than the dirt road leading to the door of the planter's house where they were told to turn around and get out. The sovereignty of the planter on his own land was never questioned before or after slave days.

The transition to a wage economy did change the Delta in some ways. Many landowners found that a practical way to avoid the use of cash was to begin sharecropping their land. It was also possible for a very industrious and fortunate few of the black workers to save enough money from the wages of a tenant farmer or the proceeds from cropping to buy sections of land. Since the 1940s, a number of small farms have been set up in Humphreys County by men raised as tenant farmers. Their owners have often helped to bring relatives off the plantations by giving them pieces of the newly acquired land to sharecrop. The planter, however, retained control, at least into the 1950s, over the independent sharecropper and the small farmer. Farming income is seasonal. If any money is to be made, it will come in the late fall and will be spent by spring. Small farmers require a "furnish," a loan to cover all farm and personal expenses for the six months of the year spent in planting and waiting for the crop. The Farmers Home Administration, which offers the same type of service to the farmer that the Federal Housing Authority does to the city dweller, has loans to serve this purpose, but in the 1940s and '50s black farmers had trouble being approved for them. While many turned to the banks for furnishing, most took the familiar path and received loans from the large planters. The practice continues today though a few small farmers have begun to take advantage of the recently relaxed policies of the FHA.

For the most part, the plantation system and the relation of tenant to planter remained basically the same from its beginnings until the late 1950s. Then, the forces of the first hallelujahs of the civil rights movement, of a northward migration again getting into swing, and of a new idea in agricultural efficiency—mechanization—converged on plantation country and began to alter the system in such a way that some day its back will be broken. But in the meantime, it will take a great toll in human suffering.

⟨ Now, I've seen the time when we'd come home from school, and we'd go into the fields, make about six bits, a dollar, picking cotton by the hundred. But in the fields now, there ain't nothin' doin'. It looks lonesome. Ain't nobody workin' in it 'cept cotton pickers. Machines— that's all it is . . . . I seen the time when we had great big long trailers about as long as this house. I'us pickin' then two-fifty, three, when I was in the prime, sometimes four. I could live. People ain't gettin' nowhere. They're just managing alone. I don't know. See what if there come a snow on these people. I don't know what we'd do—me and all the rest. We'd have to make snow bread or something.

In 1960, before the machines had completely taken over, a plantation of any size would have had ten to forty tenant families. Their shacks would have been strung along the dirt roads as little neighborhoods a half mile long, where every family drank from a single faucet by the road and often shared common outhouses. All of the people, perhaps numbering several hundred, would work every day that it did not rain throughout the spring, chopping cotton in the summer and picking cotton in the fall. The wage was poor, averaging three to five dollars a day for men and considerably less for women and children.

Today only the skilled men have jobs; manual labor has seen its day on Delta plantations. Poison sprayed from crop-dusting planes has ended the demand for cotton choppers. Mechanical cotton pickers, looking insect-like with their large awkward bins angling out above their tiny wheel base, have replaced hand pickers, except at the ends of the rows where the picker makes its turn and cannot reap cleanly for a stretch about fifteen feet deep in the row. Here the women still can get a few sacks. With the reduction of cotton allotments to southern planters and the wider use and availability of machines, soybeans, a crop that cannot be picked by hand, have begun to challenge King Cotton in the Delta. Some planters like to keep their bean fields neater than crop dusters can make them, and here again there is occasional work for the women and children.

⟨ Now the people don't live on the plantations like they used to. All the houses are tore down. Maybe on some plantations the people are living out there, and maybe on some about ten or twelve families. Then there are some plantations here that have families there that never been further than there. They've been there all their lives.

Have they been putting people off the land?

Well, I think the people moved off the land 'cause there wasn't any work to do.

When did the people first start moving out?

About in '63. Way back. Because of the machines and this new stuff they use to kill the grass.

Men too old to learn to handle machines, but who have spent their lives on the plantation, stay on by the grace of the planter and can find no work at all.

❲ Well, I don't do anythin' now. For the past six years—well I used to farm, but after I got in bad health, I started haulin' and hoein', but I ain't did a thing like that since they got to the place where they just about stopped pickin' cotton and hoein'. So I just take it easy now, I reckon.

Do you have any income?

No sir.

At least half of the tenants on the plantations around Louise do almost no work. They are women without husbands, old people, sick people, unskilled people. There is no evidence that there is everywhere a concerted drive on to evict them, yet nothing is being done to provide them with the means to stay alive.

❲ *What do you do, Mrs.———?*

Well, right now, we're pickin' cotton.

About how many months out of a year do you work?

Well right now, I'd say about two because they usually put the cotton pickers in to pick the cotton.

How much did the two of you make this week?

Ten dollars and sixty-two cents.

If you did well, would you make closer to twenty dollars?

Well no, 'cause I'm not a very good cotton picker. See, you'd have to average 200 pounds a day to make twenty dollars, and I'm not a very good cotton picker. Some days I pick eighty, some days ninety. And in the morning you can't go out early because of the dew. They don't want you to pick it when it's too wet.

The unskilled men too young to be tied down by families of their own leave the Delta and the state for the jobs in the North. In Louise, there are virtually no young men between the ages of eighteen and twenty-five. Only one or two members of each class that graduates from the black high school in Louise can still be found in the county a year later.

❲ *Do you think your children will ever come back from Chicago?*

They would come back and go to the field if they could make anything. They don't mind, my children don't mind, real work. *But,* it's just workin' and not gettin' nothin' out of it. Now when they was here, I wasn't able to give them anything. I was glad they left.

It is difficult to operate farm machines—tractors, bulldozers, cotton pickers, and combines—and difficult to run a cotton gin. A bean combine, for example, must be watched by a mechanic at all times, or be operated by an especially determined and talented driver. Parts break down; engine belts snap; the machine jams. A ginning operation must run constantly to process the flow of raw cotton at harvest, and something in a cotton gin will break every day. To operate and understand heavy farm machinery is not an easily acquired knack, and planters do not want to employ anyone who does not have it. A heavy-duty tractor (the kind commonly used in the Delta) costs a minimum of $5,000. A combine costs well over $20,000. The obvious risk of putting a barely-skilled or untrained man on a $20,000 machine has meant the birth, though not yet the maturity, of a competitive market for labor.

This does not imply that there is any bidding on the price of skilled labor. The minimum wage is everywhere the same for the tenant farmer: $1.00 an hour in 1967, $1.15 an hour in 1968, and $1.30 an hour in 1969. But some planters do try to entice tenants away by promising more work. It is hard, however, to foster competition among planters accustomed to cooperation. No planter in Louise has made any real attempt to improve the tenant homes or to invest in better machines, e.g., tractors with heated cabs, though these are the current bargaining factors in other areas and are guaranteed to attract the finest hands in the county. Real competition is still reserved for the giant plantations.

The small planters prefer to let workers come to them and ask for jobs. For a variety of reasons, including age, family, children, and tradition, most tenant farmers do not search around for jobs on the large or newly-organized plantations. The single men do, of course, and they follow the work to Florida, then to New York in the winter and spring, and back to Mississippi for planting and harvest. For the skilled tenant farmer, the new status has meant that he is now the breadwinner of the family, that he can, to a degree, bargain with the agent, that his economic utility is visibly equal to or greater than that of any white man, and, importantly, that if he cannot get enough work to do on one plantation, or is kicked off, he can usually find a new job.

The Minimum Wage Law of 1966, which for the first time set the wage for agricultural employees, dealt the death blow to unskilled labor and expendable skilled labor on the plantations. Until that time, the wage of the tenant farmer had fluctuated around three dollars a day, and women and children could work full time picking cotton on a piece-rate basis. All of these people, except the children, came under the new law and were entitled to one dollar an hour beginning in 1967. Though some planters in Louise do not pay the wage, or pay a straight time salary that falls below the minimum wage, or unfairly calculate the number of hours that their tenants work, most follow, more or less, the dictates of the law and in doing so cut from their work lists all but the essential laborers. In the case of large families, the law has had the unfortunate effect of putting the wife and older children out of work, placing the responsibility for earning money solely on the man, and while increasing his earnings, leaving unchanged the total family income.

(At first, the machines started throwin' people off the plantation, and after the wage law came along that made plantation owners buy more machines and put more people off.

❴ *What is the most pressing problem of the people here?*

Finance. Finance is the most pressing problem. The people need work to do. That's the problem: they can't find it . . . . If they leave, the people would have to have money to leave on. Well naturally, they don't have the money. If I was on the plantation and couldn't find any work to do, well I would have to leave here and try to find myself a job. I would have to have money to take me over until I found a job, and if I couldn't find a job right away I would have to turn around and come back before the little money I had run out. That's the main reason that people don't leave the plantations whenever they are displaced from work.

The tenant farmers are poor because they cannot earn enough to live on. Those who stay on the land work by the hour and work only when called upon by the agent. Some labor for "straight time," a minimal salary paid all year round. For most, there is no work when it rains, and it rains frequently in the farming season. For most, there is no work at all in the winter, and they then borrow heavily from the planter, accumulating a debt that reduces their spring and fall wage below any humane calculation of what it costs to raise a family.[1]

❴ *Do you work on the plantation?*
Yes.
What do you do?
I drive a tractor.
Is that a full-time job?

---

[1] The 1960 population of Humphreys County was 19,093. In 1966, it had fallen to 18,700. The non-white population was 65.8 per cent of the total. In 1960 there were 3,911 families in the county. According to the Social Security Administration income scale, 2,324 of the 2,493 non-white families were poor, and 484 of the 1,418 white families were poor. Thirty-five per cent of the population had failed to complete four years of school and were thus functionally illiterate. The unemployment rate in the county in 1960 was 5.9 per cent.

No sir, sure ain't.
Just part of the year?
Part of the year. I'd say just six months out of a year, six or seven good months.
How much can you make during the six months?
Oh, I don't know. About a couple thousand dollars, I reckon. Might, I doubt it.
How do you make it by the other six months?
Well, I just do the best I can.
How many people do you have living here?
Let's see. I got nine. Seven kids and my wife.

Some women work as maids or cooks or sew and quilt for neighbors. A maid in Louise is paid three dollars a day. A quilt can be sold for from three to five dollars.

❨ Before I worked for CDGM[2] I worked as a maid. I would get three dolars a day; go to work at seven, get off at any time, for my thirteen children . . . .

❨ *Do you have any income, sir?*
No sir.
Are you employed, ma'am?
I draws welfare, and sewing, that's all I do.
How much do you make from your sewing?
'Cordin' to the sewing I get. Sometimes I make four to five, six dollars per week. Sometimes I don't make nothing.
How large is your welfare check?
Fifty dollars. [a month]

❨ *Where do you work?*
I works here on the farm.
What do you do on the farm?
Oh, tractor driving. Just anything in farm work he got to do.

---

[2] Child Development Group of Mississippi, a multi-county Head Start program which employs as teachers, aides, cooks, and drivers many poor black mothers. See pp. 67–68.

About how often do you work?

Well, I works pretty often, 'cause I'm workin' for straight time, but I count it for nothin'. I make about thirty-five dollars a week, straight through the year . . . . No raise, no cut, and really I just account that for nothing. You just can't hardly get through on it. I have all my debts to pay, doctor bills, my house expenses, all that to keep up. Doctor bills, food stamps, all of that.

Did the man who owns the plantation help you with the doctor's bills?

Well, he'll stand for them, but you got to pay him. I've got to pay him out of this weekly salary that I told you about . . . . I have a certain amount that I pays if I have to have a little extra debt. I have a certain amount to pay. I live out of about twenty-five dollars a week of that money, and I take the rest of that for my little bills . . . . Naturally, you can't pay this debt right away. Pay that and live too, you see. If I had to just pay a big amount, I wouldn't live at all. Really, I get just enough to eat on.

How large is your family?

They's ten of us—five in school.

How many hours do you usually make a day?

I don't have hours. I make from sunup to sundown and sometimes an hour or two at night, this time of year haulin' cotton. Now a straight time salary it would do pretty good—if it paid enough. There's some few, some few men in this county, pays about fifty dollars a week. If I could get the work to do steady enough, on the hour basis, I'd rather by the hour, but if I go by the hour I can't feed my family 'cause I can't get the work to do. More'n generally of us will work cheap—straight time and cheap—then you gets work all the time. It's the only way you can get work to do, but you don't get nothing for your work. But if you go by the hour then they'll swear they don't have the work to do, and you'll sit down and half the time you can't keep yourself fed. You don't get nothin' in the winter at all. You don't get nothin' in the winter.

《 Well, my income is poorly. I didn't have no income further than the furnish. I get six months furnish to make the crop.

In an average year, how much do you make above the furnish?

Sometime I don't make anything.

How do you get through the last six months of the year?

Well I just have to do the best I can . . . . If it takes it all to pay what I owe, well it gets it all . . . . Before I got behind—I got behind by havin' years of short crops—before I got behind I was doing pretty good. I was making twelve, fifteen hundred dollars after I cleared up my indebtedness. But now, I haven't paid that in five years. I've been behind that long. We had three bad years. It rained and the crop was very short. So that just put me in bad shape . . . This year I *might* pay out and I might not.

The small farm owner has been plagued for the last several years with crops that just will not pay the bills. He, too, has been forced by the economics of modern agriculture to abandon most manual labor. He must own a tractor to put in the crop, and most likely will have to hire a cotton picker to get the crop in. Should he, in the face of the constantly worsening market for cotton and cotton seed, choose to plant soybeans, he will have to pay a man with a combine to harvest his crop for about 15 per cent of the market value. Since price supports are based on acreage, the small landowner gets virtually no federal help. As a landowner, he is usually considered to be too well off to receive any benefits from any programs of the welfare department, including food stamps and commodities. To buy seed, fertilizer, weed poisons, and everything else that is needed to farm he must obtain a furnish to cover all non-equipment farm expenses for the six months from planting to harvest. The furnish includes a small monthly amount for living expenses. Many small farmers cannot from year to year repay their furnishes, at the normal 6 to 8 per cent interest, from the proceeds of their crop.

((*What is your income from farming?*
My income? Well for the last two or three years, it hadn't been nothin' . . . nothin' to amount to nothin'.
Do you meet the payments on your furnish?
Well I didn't pay it last year . . . Last year I didn't make but eleven bales, and I know the way it was last year we didn't make more than $75–$80 a bale. I'll tell you the truth about how we make it. Our kids what finished school up North send us money now and then. We wouldn't make it without that.

Many are able to break even; only a few clear money above their furnish and equipment costs. While it is true that they can raise much of what they eat, their cash income is so incredibly low that in all things but food, they survive on a level at or below that of the tenant farmer.

((For the last four or five years, all of us farmers done about alike. Ain't none of us made no money on the farm . . . . We got a tractor there that we pay a note on that costs $5,700 net, nothing but the tractor, $5,700 for that tractor to farm that 120 acres of land, and we have seven years to pay for it, and we have to pay $1,000 a year. And we actually haven't made no money in the last four years. All us farmers are based just about alike.
Neighbor: Look like the little people, the little farmers, he'll have to come off the farm 'cause they can't operate no farm.

There are almost no non-farm jobs for men in Louise. Belzoni is becoming a manufacturing town, but few black men are hired by local industry. The young men, both white and black, in Humphreys County for the most part want nothing to do with farming. They look at the meager return that comes from independent farming, and the indignity and low wage that is the lot of the tenant, and they leave the county. The manufacturers in Belzoni prefer to hire whites. The blacks go to Jackson, Chicago, St. Louis, and Baltimore—the farther from the farm, the better.

(I have two boys who've left for Chicago.
Do you think they'll ever come back?
No, I don't think so. 'Cause there's nothing here for boys to do. Long time ago the children used to stay home; they could go to the fields and things. Now they don't need you in the field no more 'cause they've got this new chemistry that kills grass and the machines picks the cotton so they don't have anything here to do. No factories. I think there are two here: a garment factory and I don't know what kind of factory this is over here.

(My wife was up there trying to sign up to go to that factory, and when the turn-out came at twelve, three colored women came up and two colored men and that was all. It was just like a school turn-out, there was so many people.

(*Do you think that the one that's fourteen will stay here when he gets out of high school?*
I wouldn't think so.
Do you think he'll head North?
To make anything he's have to.

(*Do you think your children will stay in Mississippi when they get out of school?*
I don't believe so. Now and then you'll catch one who'll stay, but it all needs to be changed to keep 'em here.
What needs to be changed?
The wages got to go up. They won't stand what I'll take.

⟨ One time my wife wasn't working, and I didn't have no job. She just got a job this year. All right. All of 'em was lookin' right at me. There wasn't no food stamps out then. And I had to first just throw myself way behind—different things—just tryin' to make it. See I didn't want to get in debt. My boss told me I could borrow some money. I didn't want to borrow none this year. I didn't borrow none. I borrowed some from him last year, and I had a hard time trying to pay it back . . . . See, here the way he do. When I borrow some money from him, he won't give me no work to do. When he gives me a job to do, he'll take out the money, and that kind of puts me in strains . . . . So I swore I wasn't going to borrow no more money if I had to eat three months of cornbread. Something like that.

II **The Planter**

There are three levels of social position in the white community of Louise. Lowest are the rednecks, peckerwoods, crackers, i.e., the poor whites who are either small farmers, laborers on plantations, or blue collar workers. They are often as poor as any black man, and they suffer, as he does, the difficulties of continual indebtedness to the planter and the indignity of being excluded from participation in making decisions affecting their lives. Above the poor whites are the agents on the plantations who are responsible for seeing that the work gets done and who are paid relatively good salaries and generally provided with nice homes. They constitute a small middle class in the community, but they, too, are a group with no voice in the government of their town.

The planter governs the community. That he may or may not hold an elected office is unimportant. He exercises effective control just as certainly as does a plant manager in a small company town. Almost everyone works for him. In Louise, and elsewhere in the Delta, the interests of the plantation are the interests of the community. The planters themselves, many of whom are barely middle class by the standards of America as a whole, take on, by tradition rooted nearly two centuries deep, the role and responsibilities of the aristocracy. They act in unity—a unity which sometimes requires the expulsion from grace of one of their own—to further the economic progress of their towns, but most importantly, to maintain what is proper and good in the lives and attitudes of the people in their community. A central tenet of their view of propriety is that the races must be kept separate. To observe this command has been the life's work of many white southerners, but for most it has been the belief governing their lives: it has made sensible the alliance of rich and poor, exploiter and exploited, criminal and God-fearing, that characterizes white communities in the rural South.

There is a mayor and a city council in Louise. The councilmen with one exception are all planters, and the mayor is usually some unfortunate storekeeper who acquiesced under great pressure and accepted the position. For the twelve years prior to 1968, Louise had a Jewish mayor, the proprietor of a slowly failing grocery store.

The town officials are elected, a fact unknown to every black man interviewed: every black man in Louise with whom I talked had no idea as to how the officials got into office. Black residents call the town council "The White Citizens' Council," which it could possibly be, and they do not know whether this body is elected or privately selected. There are two polling places in Louise. Voting in county, state, or national elections is done in two makeshift stalls behind a gas station. Voting for what black people have always assumed to be the "Citizens' Council" is done at the town hall. No black man interviewed had ever walked across the street to vote in town elections. To do so would be an act of extraordinary bravery for very little return, because the man would certainly be attacked and because the "Citizens' Council," in the normal course of its business, does very little that interests or affects the black community. It is the planters' private club, and generally whites of lesser station do not know what it is doing.

The "Citizens' Council" has been credited in the past with occasional acts of meanness such as blacklisting, boycotting, threatening, or terrorizing men who challenge them. In drastic cases, they mete out almost equal treatment to white and black men alike. The president of the "Citizens' Council" is a planter. The vice-president is the town doctor. One problem that the planters have been unable to rid themselves of is that the owner of a sizeable plantation outside of Louise has for nearly twenty years been married to a black woman. He has resisted every pressure put on him by switching his ginning business to other towns, and he is reported to have been seen at night in front of his door with a gun, looking as if he'd fire at anything.

Most of the important elected offices in Humphreys County are held by plantation owners, and all appointed officials bend to the will of the planters. The chain of coercive and moral authority is thus preserved in the political as well as the social and economic spheres. One example of what this can mean is the recent conflict within the public school system. There was until the 1968–69 school year a white elementary and high school in Louise with over two hundred pupils. In 1967 Humphreys County instituted the freedom-of-choice plan for school desegregation and assigned a carefully-selected Negro teacher to Louise School. Even though no black parent chose to send his child to the white school, the hiring of the teacher caused tremendous uproar in the white community. This, added to the real possibility that some students would change schools in 1968, forced the county board of education to employ the final solution: shut down the white school and bus white children twenty miles out of their own community to Holly Bluff and Yazoo City in Yazoo County. The school building in Louise now stands empty, yet it is refused as a site for a community center or a day care center. In a tiny place like Louise the closing down of a public building for any reason is a disgrace. It was an act demonstrating unbelievable determination and dedication to old values, and it would seem madness, if the people did not accept it so naturally.

What does your husband make?
    When he's here on the place, he doesn't make but about five, six dollars a day. So that was puttin' us in a strain so he had to go off to get a job.
    About how many hours would he work for that five or six dollars?
    From six till six.
    But he's got another job now?
    He's workin' at the gin in Rolling Fork.
    What will he do in the spring?
    Work here on the place. Choppin' cotton and plowin'.
    For five dollars a day?
    When he's on the tractor. Now when he's choppin' cotton he gets four dollars.
    The planter hasn't asked you to leave yet?
    He did. Last week after my husband went off to work, he said if he could work over there he could move. So when my husband came in, he went over to talk to him Sunday morning, and he said he can't fix the house. "I ain't able to fix the house—bad a shape as that house is in. I just rather put hay in it." He told us he would like us to move so he could get hay in it. Two or three weeks, we got to move.

The tenant farmer engaged in civil rights activity has always been extremely vulnerable to the loss of his livelihood and has generally been the first to feel the wrath of the white community, though it is now a little easier to take that risk because a skilled worker can usually find work. Still, a planter with only one tenant and no prospect of running up on another would force that family to move in a minute if he heard that any member of it was engaged in what he considered to be "radical activity," which could range from registering to vote to joining the NAACP. He would do it because it made him mad. A point perhaps not yet overstated is that when people spend their lives depending upon others, the "others" do not feel like oppressors; they feel paternalistic. And, in fact, what made the plantation different from labor camps was that the planter tried to respond to the needs of his tenants as he saw them. Certainly most planters viewed the loan that they extended to get a family through the winter more as a kind act, the sort that men must perform occasionally, rather than as one link in a chain of bondage. The civil rights movement, and especially the warm reception the young northerners got from black people in the South, seemed to the planter a massive rejection of the decency with which he had tried to live his life. The kindness that might once have played a part in the relationship between planter and tenant is disappearing; it is being replaced by the callousness between management and labor.

One example of the changing times is that of the tenant's vegetable or truck garden. Until a few years ago, every family on a plantation was allowed a small patch of land to grow vegetables for its own use. Many tenants also raised hogs, chickens, and possibly a cow. Today only a few of the planters will allow even their full-time laborers to plant one or two rows of vegetables. For the rest, a garden or coops or pens for poultry and livestock are impossible because rows of cotton or soybeans now push up to the tenant's doorstep. In their drive to get the greatest possible yield from their land, the planters may force the tenants to move their toilets right up to their homes, so that every possible foot of land can be seeded and so that the machines can run straight down the rows without having to detour around the tiny, rickety privies. Even where space does permit the growing of a little truck, most tenants are prohibited from doing so because planters fear that weeds from the garden will spread to the cotton and bean fields, which they like to keep meticulously clean by spraying down poisons from the air.

Another, more important, example is the treatment accorded to families living on the plantation where the man is too old to work or there is no man to work. It is in the tradition of the plantation system that a tenant who had spent his life working on the place would be guaranteed a little bit of work here and there as long as he was able and a minimal sort of old-age security—a house to remain in until he died, occasional loans to see him through the winter, and help in paying medical expenses. What the planter could not provide, the family or neighbors of the old man or husbandless mother might contribute. Now it is likely that a man has few neighbors and that most of his family has left the Delta. There is virtually nothing, not even makework, for the old, unskilled, or female to do on the plantation. And now, try as they may, no tenants not working regularly can believe the boss who says, "You can live here as long as you need to." They have seen too many families, believing the same promise, who were told one afternoon to leave by the next morning so that the house into which they were born could be burned and planted over in cotton.

Plantation income in the best of times is relatively unpredictable. Farming is a hazardous occupation, and men can be laid up for weeks with broken arms and legs. Whenever it rains no work can be done, and when the crop is bad everyone suffers. Yet always before, a family in trouble would not go unaided by its neighbors on the plantation, and, too, the plantation owner could be counted upon to help in difficult times if only by offering his tenant a loan. The plantation was a community in which the planter held the ultimate authority and in which each member felt common problems and common burdens. The community is now being destroyed. Each man's plight is different from that of the rest. Class distinctions, between skilled and unskilled, are being created within the ranks of the tenant farmers. The power of the planter is not guarding over them; it is seemingly aimed directly at them.

The planter is out to make money, and, viewed in this way, he is coming of age.[3] The last years in the Delta have seen tenants go homeless, truck patches on plantations prohibited or restricted, people dying or being permanently disabled because the planter would not send for a doctor, plantation huts being allowed to fall into complete disrepair, women and children by the thousands left with no way to earn money, women forced to do work for which they are physically unsuited in order to save their families from being told to move out, and countless other shameful events. This has happened, I think, not because the planters have decided to starve the black man out of the Delta, as some have said, but rather because the planters no longer care, except as it affects their own operations, what happens to the tenants on their farms; or in a larger sense, they do not care whether the black man in the Delta starves or not.

There is nothing predictable now about life on the plantation. No man knows if his home is secure, or if he will be given enough work to support his family. He does not know if he will be placed in a hospital if he is hurt on the job. He has no idea what he will do when he becomes too old to

[3] In 1967 seventy-two planters in Humphreys County received cash payments for land in the soil bank in excess of $20,000 a year. Six planters received cash payments of more than $100,000 a year. The largest planter in Louise received $133,764. Nine planters received between $50,000 and $100,000 a year.

work. If he falls into debt to the planter, he does not know if he will be given enough work to get in the clear. He can no longer expect the planter to give him materials with which to repair his house. If he owes the planter or cannot accumulate any savings, he has no way to leave the plantation. If he can contemplate leaving, he, who has never been one hundred miles from Louise, must face a move to Chicago which he has seen on television but does not really believe in. And what will he do in Chicago? The plantation world is all uncertainty, and the tenant farmer is economically and politically unable to make it any less so.

Those who for years, for all of their lives, have carried upon their shoulders the weight of crying, underfed children, increasing debt to "the man," and diminishing return for their labor, have a near total and perhaps unique dependency on the planter who has found himself, over the last years, labeled as an oppressor and who today, it is feared, has decided to live up to the title. The old dependency is a bond that now, when things are terribly difficult for the tenant farmer in Mississippi (and it cannot often enough be emphasized that each year the situation worsens), makes the tenant helpless to stand and fight back and unequipped to handle the role of independent laborer now imposed upon him. As an independent laborer, the tenant farmer is quickly replaceable, if not altogether dispensable; he is no longer a member of the community that was the plantation. The fear of what will be has taken hold; it has sent the young people fleeing north, and the old people wondering where to turn.

◖ *Does he (the planter) ever do anything to fix the place up?*

Well, I moved here with him last year a little before

Christmas. He put some window casings in and some windows in this old house. Old house ain't had anybody livin' in it for about five years. There's every kind of insect in it now that's in that swamp down there . . . . I laid down one night, and when I went to bed there wasn't anything wrong with that hand. I woke up the next morning, it had a knot on it. And from that it inflamed some more. It just had a little knot there—just like the end of your thumb—and that place inflamed and got sore, and course it was right on the hand and drivin' the tractors that kept it worked up . . . . And that place was sore when they treated my head about a month ago. Course, I put it to a spider bite.

Do any of your children keep catching colds all winter?

Well, they catch them that way. I feel like they catches them from the houses I live in that's not capable to live in. See, I've got to keep in the heater, when it's cold, a red hot fire. Well, to get the house hot, you have to get it too hot to live in it, see. And you get it hot and in thirty minutes it's cool, and you've already picked up a moist of sweat. That's the way I figure my kids catch so many colds . . . . You can get one real hot settin' up over that heater, and I guarantee he'll catch a cold. Your house is not built right. Just in a few minutes after your fire die out, your house is cold. And supposin' the walls is open—the air blowin' right in on you.

III   Household

In order to comprehend a man's poverty, it is not always necessary to document what he eats and what he earns. All one needs to do is to see the house in which he lives. In Humphreys County, the tenants refer to their homes as "open houses," which means that the walls are full of holes covered by cardboard, that there is no sealing (no inner layer to the walls), that the window frames hold no glass and are covered with sheets of tin, that the ground can be seen through the floor boards, that both rain and snow come in the roof and that wind blows through the house all night. Most people heat their homes with wood burned in a fireplace or in an old cast iron heater. If they leave a fire when they go to bed, the house is colder than outdoors by the time they are asleep. If they like to keep a fire going all night then they must get out of bed every hour to add wood and re-light the heater and will probably have to run outside into the freezing night to fetch more wood. There is danger involved in trying to stay warm all night. In the old rickety heaters with worn tin chimneys, a fire long unwatched can blaze too hot, sending sparks popping through the flue and threatening the whole house. The tragedy of being burned out has struck many families in Louise.

Since most black people around Louise live on plantations, most of them do not own their own homes. A fact often ignored in better days, it has now become painfully significant. One way in which it affects living conditions is that now, when the planter will do nothing to repair and maintain the homes of any but his indispensable workers, most tenants, having no job security whatsoever, are left wondering whether they dare invest money in fixing up a house that they may soon lose. It is worth noting that many tenant homes date back fifty years, and that the wood with which they were constructed came from houses which had at that time collapsed. They have seen many generations of many families. When a tenant's home burns or falls down, or when he moves on to a new plantation, he must take whatever vacant house he can find. The home into which he moves may have stood empty for months, years, or even decades. Thus, when a family takes a new house, they must first battle to reclaim the fragile wooden shell from the weeds, rot, rats, mice, rubbish, snakes, and small animals that have accumulated or moved in over the years. One company in the Louise area has constructed sixteen very nice tenant homes on its land. The company, however, is not based in Mississippi and bought the plantation only three years ago. The indigenous planters have generally made little attempt to bring the shacks of the day laborer up to any standard of decency.

❨ *Do you think your children are about as healthy as they could be?*

No I don't think they're so healthy on account of I can't give them sufficient food and put sufficient rainments on them like they're supposed to be. You have to have shoes and clothes and a warm shelter. Well, you see, they ain't got that. See we've been here ten years, and I buy paper every year to keep warm, but it don't do any good.

Do any of your floors have holes in them?

They ain't no good. Ain't no good.

What happened to your porch out there?

It's tryin' to get away.

❨ *Is there anything in your house that needs fixing up real bad?*

Just to tell it like it is, the whole thing needs fixin' up if that's what you want to know.

We need a house built, let alone fix it.

I don't know whether you could fix this trap.

The man who owns the place, does he charge any rent?

If he did I wouldn't live here.

What would you do?

I'd go somewhere else.

Neighbor: Ain't worth it.

Ain't worth it.

Neighbor: Ain't worth bein' here as it is.

That's right.

Is your porch in good shape?

Neighbor: It's worser than the house.
Sure enough.[4]

❨ This house doesn't have any cinders under it. This back part is setting on the ground. The only thing that's holdin' it up are the blocks on the front part. In the daytime you can mostly see how it slants—this part here up and that part there down.

The floors in most homes are full of holes. Usually there are areas in the corners of the floor and around the fireplace where it is unsafe to step. Heavy items, such as deep freezers, even if they could be afforded, cannot be installed in some homes because the floors will not support them.

❨ *Do you use this fireplace for heat?*
Yes.
You don't have a heater?
No. Now this place right here [in front of the fireplace], it ain't nothin' but the ground. See it broke in right in here, and the fireplace fell in. It decayed all in here and it ain't nothin' but the ground. It's full of dirt. We filled it in.

❨ *Do any of your floors have holes in them?*
Husband: Look here. Don't you see how it is?
Wife: It's a wonder you ain't falled through none of them.
Husband: House ain't no good.

After the crop is brought in, rats and mice will come out of the fields and invade the tenants' homes searching for food. Snakes and spiders follow them up through the holes in the floors.

❨ *Are you bothered by rats, snakes in the house?*
Yeah, rats runnin' all over the place.

---

[4] James McBride Dabbs has described southerners as "piazza people," dwelling in a sort of cool half-life between the unbearable introspective privacy of "indoors" and the irreconcilable injustice of the public life beyond the porch. Porches are, then, inordinately important to southerners.

Have they ever bitten anybody?

One bit my wife a week ago on the foot. It was a mice.

It was the night I was trying to get my reports[5] out, and I was sittin' on the edge of the bed and something bit me. I first thought it was one of the kids under there and then I screamed.

❮ *Do you ever have any problems with snakes or rats in your house?*

We have rats. Plenty of rats.

Is there anything you can do to keep rats from getting in?

Well sometimes we put down poison for them— some kind of poison we put down—but then we be scared to use that on parts of the children. They might get hold to it.

❮ *Is there anything you'd like to talk about . . . ?*

Oh yes sir, I sure would love an indoor toilet. I sure would.

I always wished for a house that I could live in and wouldn't be bothered with the rats and snakes comin' in. We had two snakes come in here year before last. The house ain't been too good till last year. We repaired it.

❮ Rats and roaches like to eat me up.

Of the families surveyed 76.6 per cent are troubled by rats in their homes, and 23.4 per cent of the families have killed snakes in their homes.

The sealing of a house, one man said, is like the undershirt on a man. It is protection against wind and cold. None of the houses of the poor black farmers in Louise is well sealed. Some have no sealing at all. In houses where a wooden inner wall was once built, it has long since begun rotting and falling apart, and only cardboard and tin hold out the wind. "Beaverboard," a thick cardboard, and "brick

[5] The mother of the family works at a Head Start center. Her job requires her to keep accounts of attendance and expenditures.

paper," a heavy wallpaper, are used in tenant houses where wooden sealing never was installed. Neither is particularly durable, and again, torn up cartons provide most of the protection from the elements. The walls in many houses are covered with newspaper to patch the tiny cracks, but nothing really works. In houses this old, the wind will find its way past whatever men put up to stop it.

❲ *Does the rain come in the roof?*
Well no, it doesn't leak. With the understanding— the sealing and the outside walls, in the winter, ain't no account at all. These here, all these swollen places, see that's wind cracks where the wind comes through there. If you didn't plaster the paper over that, you see, it'd come right on in. Well naturally it do come in in places. Paper pushed away and all like that, well the wind did that.

❲ *Are your walls sealed?*
No sir. We're outdoors. We're outdoors. If it was daylight you could just see all those—around the edges there—holes.
They ain't no account, these old houses. They ain't fixed this house in five years.

In summer the rain comes through the roof. In winter, snow will settle lightly on the living room floor and on the beds.
There are always more people than there are beds in a household. In some homes the children must sleep wrapped in blankets on the floor. Where there are beds, the children sleep two, three, and four in each. On summer nights, when the air is heavy and hot, the children often prefer the floor to their overcrowded beds.

❲ *Where do the children sleep? In beds?*
In beds.
Do any sleep on mats on the floor?
Two.

How many are in the beds?
Three in one bed, two in the other. The baby sleeps
with us.

◖ *How many rooms do you have to sleep in here?*
Two. It ain't much for 'em to sleep.
*So all eight of the children sleep in one of the two
beds?*
Well, they share.

The children sleep an average of 2.2 in each bed. There
are never enough blankets or quilts in the wintertime. The
children sleep with their clothes on and with coats and
sweaters laid over them. Thirty per cent of the families ad-
mit to not having enough blankets in the winter.

Wood, gas, and coal are burned to heat the homes. Wood,
the traditional fuel, costs four to six dollars for a load that
will last about a week in the winter. The working men chop
their own wood; the women and old men buy theirs. A
family of women and children living alone with no neighbors close by is entirely dependent on the punctuality of the
wood dealer and on whether or not he can pass on the roads.
He is sometimes late, and the family stays cold. So do the
ones who cannot pay for the wood at all. Gas heaters are
safer, more economical, and more trustworthy than wood
heaters, but the cost of buying them and installing the
tanks is too high for most people.

◖ I got a gas stove and I burn wood in the wintertime,
and the house ain't fit to live in. Ain't got no sealing in it
nowhere. Just one wall sittin' up there. I buy wood all
winter long.
What does the wood cost you?
I pay twenty dollars a month to buy wood. It costs
five dollars a load, and I burn four loads a month.

◖ And that house. I like to froze last year. Wonder we,
me and her, both ain't dead. I like to froze. I went on

to the grudge ditch one morning. I prayed a good prayer that morning. I just did make it back to the house. I like to *froze*.

Why is it you say you almost froze? You couldn't buy the wood?

I didn't have the money. And when I did get some wood it wouldn't last a week. Couldn't nobody hardly get in there to bring no wood. And sometimes people, so many people, out of wood that they have to just go around as far as they could.

Water pipes do not run far out in the country, and even those with access to the pipes do not have running water. On the plantations the tenant families most often get their water from a common hydrant, which may be as far as a quarter mile from their homes, and the families are charged by the year for the use of the faucet. Most independent and share farmers have wells, but they are usually so shallow that the water is not good to drink. Everyone collects rain water to wash with. For drinking and washing clothes, the people must buy water by the barrel, which creates another major expense. The barrel itself costs $2.00; it costs twenty-five cents to fill it and fifty cents to have it hauled to the house. It can cost a family $1.50 (or $5.50 if their barrels are rusted out) to buy the bare minimum of two barrels of water a week. Well water is used for bathing. To bathe from a foot tub in an unheated kitchen in the middle of winter is an act of courage.

The only black people with inside toilets in Louise are a few who have houses that were built for white families in the town or the tenant farmers lucky enough to live in what the grander plantations once used for the maid's quarters. For every family interviewed who had an inside toilet, there was one who had no toilet at all.

❨ *Where is your bathroom?*
I'm rentin'.

Do you have one out back?
Sure ain't. They said they was going to build me one.

Some homes in Louise have no electricity, and some are wired for lights but the family has never been able to afford to have them turned on. On many plantations, the light bills of the tenants are sent to the planter who pays them and, once a year, adds the total bill to the debt of the tenant.

❲ *Who owns the house?*
I'm rentin'.
How much does he charge you for rent?
Eight dollars per month.
Do you have any electricity here? Lights or anything?
There's some electricity here, but it's got to be paid. I got to pay for it to be hooked up, and I ain't got the money to pay for it.

Many families do not have a table to eat on. Almost no families have enough chairs for everyone to sit and eat together. Instead they eat standing up, or sit on old molasses drums, or on the floor. Nor can everyone eat from a plate of his own. If they do not all eat from the same plate at the same time, they must wait until the one before finishes or eat out of pans and pickle jar tops.

❲ *Does everybody eat out of the same plate?*
Well I use some tops. Boiler tops. See I use a right smart of boilers. You put them on the fire and they burn up. So I save the tops.

❲ *Do you have enough plates or dishes so that everyone can eat at once?*
No I sure don't.
What do you use for plates?
Bottle tops.

❲ *Do you have enough plates and dishes to eat out of?*
Sure don't. Most I have is pans for the children to eat out of. Don't have any plates, and not many spoons, forks,

and knives. I never have been able to buy such things as
that.

It is the responsibility of the county to maintain county
roads and build bridges across the ditches that run beside
the roads. Some of the roads and drives to the houses are
in such bad shape that, when it rains, school buses cannot
get near the houses and mothers must hoist their children
up onto their shoulders and wade with them out to the bus
or simply keep them home from school. It is a struggle for
a black man to get a bridge built to his home and then to
get the county to keep it in good repair. Easy access to
paved or well-graveled roads is the privilege of the planter.

◖ Unemployed woman: There's something else I'd
like to say about Mississippi. The roads. The roads super-
visor won't fix the roads. It's a mud hole from that road
out there down to my house, and my children in the wintertime when it rains can't get out. The small ones well,
I put 'em on my back and tote 'em on up to the stop.
They won't even fix the roads . . . . I begged that man to
put some gravel on that road to fill it up, but he just won't
do it.

◖ *Is there anything in your house that needs fixing up
real bad?*

Well a lot of the windowpanes is out. I don't think
there nair' a one in that room there. When it get real
cold, we'll scrap a piece of tin and nail up there. In the
summertime it been so hot we tear it off and tack some
old screen on it. These farmers don't do anything to fix
up the house any more. It don't look like none of it's
like it should be.

When it rains the children can't get out to school.
Sometimes they be at home for two weeks. The bus
don't come down here. They have to walk out to that
road . . . . but where they have to turn in to come down
here off the blacktop, well all that's dirt road. Sometimes
when they stand in it they can't get out.

There are never enough clothes to stay warm in the winter. On very cold days, mothers keep their children home from school rather than send them out to the bus without an overcoat. Most children have but one change of clothing and often have no underwear at all. Children miss weeks of school because their mothers will not send them improperly dressed, and later they drop out of school because they cannot buy decent clothes.

 Do your children have enough clothes to get through the winter?
   No sir. I won't tell you no story. That's my puzzle: clothes and shoes and money. Schoolin' wear. I have three to go to school every day. Sometimes I have to stop them to help me a little on my job.

 I'll be lucky to near about give 'em lunch every day. But I don't know how long it's going to last. We're all what you say, naked. We don't have the proper change in clothes. Things like that. Well, it'll get cold, and the lunches'll have to stop. I'm gonna have to scrap clothes. Some way or somehow. These secondhand houses or something. I've just got to have them. We all is.

 Do you have enough clothes for your children?
   I don't have enough. We make do with what we got. We do what we be able.

Children wear out shoes quickly. The poor man cannot afford to buy a pair of new shoes for his children each time the old ones fall apart. Instead he buys, on credit, secondhand shoes that wear out before they are paid for. Some mothers will keep their kids in school no matter what they have to put on their feet. Most children, however, miss school regularly, because they own no shoes fit to wear.

 Do you have enough shoes for all of your children to go to school in?
   Well, I haven't been able to get no shoes yet. Some-

times the girl she'll send us some money for shoes, but she hasn't done it yet.

❨ *Have you ever had to pull a child out of school because he didn't have shoes?*
I had one last year.
How long did he have to stay out?
About a month.

❨ *Is there ever a time when you have to pull kids out of school because they don't have shoes?*
Sure. I have to stop mine sometimes three and four days at a time. And when I get a pair of shoes, I get a used pair. I have got them, and sometimes it'll be a couple of weeks payin' for 'em down at the secondhand store in Louise. Sometimes you can charge them, but you can't get more than one pair charged at a time. They got to see if they'll get paid for that one 'fore they'll charge you with another pair. Then you get a pair, and the kids wear 'em to school, and the soles liable to come off that same day . . . . It's pretty tough in this state.

❨ *Do all your children have shoes?*
Oh, I need to buy a pair now.
Have you ever had to take your kids out of school because they didn't have shoes?
Yes.
How long would they have to stay out?
About three or four days.

❨ You take last year. They's out of school on parts if they didn't have sufficient things to go in.
How long were they out?
They's out I reckon about a month 'fore I could get them straightened out into first going. 'Fore I could get 'em started to going.

❨ *How is your house heated?*
It's heated pretty good in the winter until the door comes open.
Do you have enough clothes for your children?
No, I sure don't.

Do you have enough for the winter?
Sure don't.
Are there enough shoes for the children?
No. They sure ain't got no shoes. Nothin' but these tennis.
Are there ever times when they don't have shoes to go to school in?
Sure is. Sometimes I have to keep 'em at home until I can get them some.
How long would they have to stay out?
About a week or so.

The children of 64.3 per cent of the families cannot regularly attend school because they have no shoes.

There are no federal or state standards to regulate the living conditions on the plantations, e.g., there is no agency empowered to say whether or not an outhouse shared by three families is sanitary, or whether a planter who will not provide a tenant with any toilet at all is acting in the interest of the public health. In 1960, only 21.4 per cent of the dwelling units in Humphreys County were sound: 58 per cent had no inside water; 73 per cent had no flush toilets; 79 per cent had no bathtubs; 43 per cent had no access to public water or an individual well; 57 per cent had no access to a public sewer, septic tank, or cesspool. There is no program of inspecting the homes that planters provide for their tenants to ensure that they are fit for habitation.[6]

❲ Yes sir, the house is got to be cured.

[6] Fifty-one of 73 families interviewed did not have enough blankets for the winter; children in 45 of 70 families missed school because of lack of shoes; 65 of 83 families responding did not have enough clothes for the winter. Only 32 of 70 families interviewed sat in chairs at a table when they ate; 25 of 85 families did not have enough dishes for everyone. Seventy-two of 94 families interviewed had holes in the floors of their homes; 77 of 92 were bothered by rats. Sixty-one of 91 homes were heated by woodstoves, 30 by gas heaters. Of 67 houses, 2 had "inside water," 15 had wells; families in 25 of the 67 houses got water from hydrants; 25 families bought water. Of 90 families interviewed, 7 had inside toilets, 76 had outside toilets, and 7 families had no toilet at all.

❲ *How many days a week do you have fresh meat?*
Just one. On Saturday.
How about fish?
Oh we seldom ever have fish. Fish man used to come by, but he stopped comin' cause the people stopped buyin'.
Do you ever eat eggs?
Yes sir.
How often will you have eggs?
Well about once a week.
How much milk do you buy in a week?
Well we don't buy by the week—just when we take a notion with the cash and got the cash. Every time I get the check, I get a little milk.
What did you have for your meals today?
Wife: Not hardly anythin'.
Husband: Had some pintos. I'm gonna tell it like it is. No meat in 'em.
Is that all you had to eat today?
Yes sir.

IV   Food and Diet

The abysmal poverty of the people turns their lives into a never-ending search for food. Getting something to eat, getting something to feed the family, is the overriding concern of the poor farmer; all other things are neglected for the sake of buying food. Groceries, in a more real sense than money, become the medium of exchange. Produce and home-produced meat are swapped for basic services such as hair cutting and auto repair work. It has been said that the case for the existence of "hunger" in the Delta has been overstated. For a family to go hungry for a long period means that they have no access to any federal food programs and that all of their neighbors and friends who would normally share what they had are in a similar situation. For a family to go hungry means that the entire community is going hungry. It means that there does not exist the means to bake or buy a loaf of bread to stuff down the mouths of the children. Most families can beg or buy that loaf of bread. But the real question is whether what people eat is adequate to support decent human life, or whether the normal diet of the people in Mississippi, in Louise, is one which the more comfortable in this nation are willing to let other Americans exist upon. Indeed, there are people in the Delta who are never free of the pain of hunger, as represented by shriveled children with swollen bellies. And certainly the very presence of cases such as these, and they are by no means rare, is horrifying enough to justify any display of fury and indignation which they arouse.

Far from the "meat and potatoes" of the "average" American, the staples of the poor farmer in Louise are pump water and pinto beans. In good seasons, pinto beans will alternate with other vegetables, string beans, sweet potatoes, turnip greens, and occasionally with chicken backs or necks. In the winter, pinto beans will alternate with white bread and molasses. Most families serve two meals at home: one in the morning and one in the late afternoon.

(We had some beans, some pinto beans. We had pinto beans for dinner. For breakfast it was toast and an egg, I think, and some bologna.

(I think we had some peas. Sure did. That's what we had. We had some green peas what she put up in the deep freezer. That's all. You know we don't have money enough to have a little of this and a little of that and the other. We don't have money for that. Sometimes we just have one thing and some bread. That's the truth.

❴ We had mashed potatoes and bread today. This morning we had eggs and light bread.

❴ Greens, collard greens, baked potatoes, and cornbread.

❴ We had some peas.

Most people can afford to eat meat only on the weekends. They eat fish about once every six weeks. Perhaps the children will be given a little fruit every other week. Because the price of eggs has gone up so high, most families are able to serve them only about three times in two weeks.

❴ *Are you ever able to buy fresh meat for your family?*
Sure do. Sometimes I do.
How many days a week would you eat meat?
Sometimes I eat it two days a week. Sometimes not at all. I don't eat it that often.
Do you ever buy fish?
No, sure don't buy no fish at all.
How about eggs?
Sometimes . . . Just when I happen to have them.
Do you ever buy fresh fruit?
Yes, sometimes I do.
Are you able to buy enough milk for your children?
Sometimes I get a quart; and sometimes I get two quarts.
Are you usually able to buy a quart every week?
No, sir, I sure ain't.

❴ *Do you ever buy fresh meat?*
No.
How about fresh fish?
I don't know. I haven't had that in so long a time.
Do you ever buy eggs?
Well, no. [She explained they get some eggs from chickens.]
Are you able to buy enough milk for your children?
I buys a little bit, but I can't buy it all the time.
How often do you buy it?
About three or four times a month.

How much do you buy when you buy it?
About a pint.
What did you have for your meals today?
I had some string beans and white potatoes.
Do you usually have the one meal a day?
No, two. Just two.
What did you have for breakfast this morning?
I had an egg.

⟨ *What did you have for your meals today or yester-day?*
Well, we had butterbeans. I don't hardly eat no breakfast.

⟨ *Do you ever have fruit?*
Very seldom. Every Christmas mostly.

Only the children in Head Start regularly eat a meal between seven in the morning and five at night. It is a treat for a child to be given the fifteen cents he needs to buy a hot lunch at school. It is not unusual for a child to have bread and syrup in the morning, or no breakfast at all, and wait until dark to have bread and syrup for supper.[7]

---

[7] Of 93 families interviewed, 10 ate meat daily; 7 ate meat three or four days a week; 19, two to three days a week; 40, one to two days a week; 3 families had meat one or two days a month; 9 families ate meat "rarely"; and 5 families "almost never" ate meat. Of 91 families interviewed, 86 had fresh fruit one or two days a month, "rarely," or "almost never." Of 90 families responding, 17 had eggs one or two days a week; 13, two to three days a week; 9, three or four days; 15 had eggs daily. Three families had eggs one or two days a month; 21 had them "rarely"; 12 families "almost never" had eggs.
   Of the 89 families responding, 4 bought three or more gallons of milk per week; 13 families bought two gallons a week; 25 bought between one gallon and one quart per week; 9 bought up to a quart a week. Four families bought up to a quart per month; 5 rarely bought milk; and 29 families bought no milk at all.
   Out of 70 families interviewed, 20 (representing 73 children) were able to afford lunch at school daily for their children; 8 families (representing 33 children) were able to give their children lunch at school three or four days a week; the 103 children of 20 families ate lunch at school two or three days a week; 56 children of 10 families ate lunch one or two days a week; the 9 children in one family ate lunch at school one or two days a month; 54 children belonging to 11 families "rarely or never" ate lunch at school.

❨ *Your children in school, do they get lunch every day?*
Wife: Not all days.

Husband: I have seven children goin' to school practically every day. Two of 'em goin' to that little school around there. It's the kindergarten school—The Friends of the Children[8]—and the others are goin' to the public school . . . . Some mornings we don't be able to get them anything. Sometimes my wife will fix them a lunch to carry along with them. We won't be able to give them anything here in the winter.

❨ *How often can your children in school buy lunches?*
Wife: To tell you the truth, you just can't manage.
Husband: That lunch. That really is a problem.
Do they buy milk at school?
They buys milk when they haves the money. It's four cents.
How often can you give them the money?
Not too regular, 'cause most times we don't hardly have the money to care for them. We just give them a nickel or things like that.

❨ *Are any of your students who can eat no breakfast, buy no lunch, and who work in crowded homes able to do well in school?*
A student would have to be especially dedicated and intelligent to get good marks under these conditions.
[assistant principal of a black high school in Belzoni]

The coming of winter carries with it the threat of starvation for many families in Louise. The least affected by the ending of the crop season are those, of course, who have regular non-farm jobs and those who receive welfare, social security, or veterans' checks, or are paid "straight time" on a plantation. But for the tenant, sharecropper, and small farmer, there is, from mid-November until April, no money coming in. To get through the winter he must borrow from

[8] The Friends of the Children of Mississippi is a four-county Head Start program administered, locally, by poor people. See pp. 67ff.

the planter and buy on credit from the stores. He will often have to share food with his neighbors; any hogs or cows straying loose on the roads are considered fair game by the first hungry man that comes along.

It is one of the luxuries of the small farmer that he can raise a garden. Throughout the autumn, he will pack away peas, beans, and tomatoes in his deep freeze to have something to fall back on in the winter. Most farmers raise hogs, and they will slaughter a shoat or hog late in the fall so that the family may enjoy a little meat occasionally in the long cold months. Some tenant farmers are accorded the privilege of planting a small garden and some are allowed to raise hogs. The greater number of tenants, however, are not allowed gardens, or have such restrictions placed upon the size of them that too little can be grown to make it practical to invest in a deep freeze. Many tenants are forbidden to raise livestock, though the cost of raising hogs prohibits most from wanting to in any case. Very few poor farmers can afford to own a cow because federal and state agencies require each cow to have a barrage of expensive vaccinations to ensure that it is free of disease. The black residents of Louise do not eat well, they do not eat much, and they do not eat often.

❨ *Does anybody in your family have high blood?*
I have a touch of it.
How about sugar diabetes?
Well, my little boy, what I was tellin' you about, he was born with this sweet blood the doctor said, and he has epileptic spells, and they sent him to Jackson and they gave him medicine for it.
Do any of your children catch colds and keep them pretty much all winter long?
Yes sir. I got some that way now. My baby . . .

*Do any of your children develop sores or scabs on
their arms and legs?*

Lord. There's some broke out here. My baby got
them worms. The doctors says it's ringworms, and she's
kinda breakin' out around her neck.

Have any ever had their stomachs bloated out?

Yes sir. The doctor said it's worms. He keeps sayin'
it's worms.

*Have any of the other children with something wrong
inside of them ever seen a doctor?*

I got another girl in there. The doctor said she had
thin tissue. When she was six months old (she's fourteen
now), I like to lost her. Said she had it so long that the
food she's given like to pass right back through her. Said
her intestines like to grow together. I have a lot of trouble
out of her for that.

V Health

The health of the people of Louise is incredibly poor.
The community is ridden with sickness, disease, and chronic
illness. While people's low income severely limits the
medical care they may receive, many find themselves often
living in the doctor's office. ("I'm just a doctor victim. I
stays in the doctor's.") Barely a household is free of a case
of high blood pressure, which shows itself in the swollen
ankles of the women, results in a weakened heart, fainting
spells, "nervous breakdowns," and demands an abstinence
from pork. Throughout the winter the children are plagued
by colds that turn occasionally into pneumonia. Cases of
asthma are not rare. Running sores and scabs dot the bodies
of most children in the summer. While often a symptom
of a dietary deficiency, they are caused in the main by unsanitary conditions which turn tiny cuts into painful infec-
tions. Diabetes is a common disease. Cases of tuberculosis

and amoebic dysentery are not hard to find. Many children
have a variety of internal parasites.[9]

⟨ This baby right here; he'll cough and go out of
breath, and you can't disturb him. He'll go out of breath.
I don't seem to know what makes him do that. If you
make him over-average mad, if he thinks you scold him
some way or the other, he'll just go right out of breath.
Sometimes it don't look like he'll get his breath back no
way. That child there, she complains right smart about
her stomach, and I taken her out to Belzoni to the doctor.
Well the doctor said she might have worms and he gave
me some worm medicine for her, but I don't know if she
was taking it like she should have 'cause I was trying to
go to school in order to pay him . . . Sometimes they
[sores] just break out all over in the summertime. I've got
another boy here who looked like he just never would get
well cf his sores.

People visit doctors most often for "high blood" pills and
for cold medicine for the children. For matters more or less
serious than these, the expense of treatment is beyond the
reach of the poor man; he would prefer to suffer through
the illness or resort to home remedies. There is not in the
Delta the hearty farm family of American folklore, living
simply but comfortably and enjoying robust good health;
instead there are people blighted by low income, inadequate
food, and disease.

There were many complaints in the interviews that people
were unable to get doctors to come to their homes, even as
in the cities.

⟨ We ain't been checked by a doctor in so long I
can't tell you what condition the family's in.

[9] Over 57 per cent of families interviewed complained of heart disease or
high blood pressure; 7 per cent had diabetes; 9.3 per cent reported that a
member of the family had asthma; 2.1 per cent had tuberculosis; 51.8 per
cent reported frequent or continuous colds; members of 59.7 per cent of
all families complained of sores or scabs on their bodies; 21.4 per cent of
the families had family members who were continually tired or listless.

About 13 per cent of the black community in Louise has never seen a doctor. Also, about 49 per cent of the people have never seen a dentist. Due to the cost, people only see dentists when their teeth need to be pulled, and when that point is reached, many people choose to pull their own teeth.[10]

❲ *How many of your children have ever seen a doctor?*
    I've got one in the family. It wasn't from sickness though. Had a little fat boy of mine. He went out to the outside bathroom one day. When he got ready to come back in, he went to zip up his pants, and he caught hisself in the zip. I taken him to the doctor. It was on a Wednesday; he takes Wednesday off, and you can't get him back to that office. So when I got to his office, he was gone. I never did try to go to his home to get him. We have a pretty favorable doctor up there in Midnight. He's real old; he'll practice till a certain hour in the evenin' and then he's through. Well, I went up there and his hours was up. Well I just kep' a goin' then. I went to Belzoni to take him to the hospital—I couldn't afford to wait because he's sufferin'—and they got it off.

There were numerous complaints about the federally-supported hospital in Belzoni. The people said patients, even emergency cases, not able to produce cash have been denied admission to the hospital and directed to hospitals in Vicksburg and Jackson where some cost reductions are granted to indigent patients. Stories were told of suffering and death resulting from the drive to these cities, each seventy miles away.

[10] Twenty-one of 36 respondents were too sick to work; 44 of 85 heads of households reported that some or all of their children had colds all winter; 49 of 82 said that their children had sores; 15 of 70 had children who were sleepy or listless all day; 45 of 81 respondents reported that a member or members of the family "often felt like fainting."
One hundred forty-eight of the 690 people in the families interviewed had never seen a doctor; 532 had never seen a dentist.

❝ I worked there at the hospital a long time. I worked over there about six or eight years. Now the hospital has changed a whole lot 'cause when I was over there we was gettin' $14 a week—go to work at seven, get off at five . . . . They take in black patients. Some, but it is so high over there that black people just can't pay it, and if you go in there and don't have the money, well, you have to go somewhere else . . . . I know a cousin of mine, on the Fourth of July, she had a miscarriage, and they carried her over there, and they wouldn't take her in. They had to rush her to Vicksburg and operate on her at once. Now, that could have been a life saved. At this hospital, you have to have money . . . . When I was there, they kept them [babies] separate . . . . The black babies stay in the nursery for a while, and then they bring them up and puts them in the diet kitchen, you know, on the colored side. Now that's what they were doing when I was there. I don't know what they're doing now.

As far as the wards are concerned, the hospital consists of, I think, thirty-four rooms that is used by patients, and eight of those rooms is used by black patients. . . . I wouldn't say they handle them any different, but it's seldom they handle any black patients. If you go to the hospital to have anything done, they will always refer you to another hospital—Jackson or Vicksburg.

The cost of medicine is one of those expenses that nags endlessly at a poor man. The shots or pills needed to check diabetes, the pills needed for high blood pressure, the non-prescription pills and syrups needed to fight the colds all winter are items which cut unbearable holes in the budget of the black man in the Delta. It is a bitter joke for a tenant farmer to pay ten dollars for an examination that shows he has "high blood" and must pay four dollars each month of his life for pills. The money is just not there. Rather than follow the doctor's instructions, he will buy, if he is able, a month's supply of pills and make them last six months.

◖ *Do you have to take medicine regularly for your sugar or high blood?*

Sure does. Course I'm not able to buy the sugar pills. I take the shots or either take the sugar pills. And I'm not able to get the sugar pills . . . .

Because they're too expensive?

Too expensive. And the doctor put me in on health department sugar shots, and the lady wrote and told me to come up there, and said the government said I'd have to pay fifty cents a week to take this treatment. And I wasn't able to pay fifty cents a week. And I didn't ever go back, and that was last year. So I have to go to the doctor in Midnight, and I haven't been there in three, four months, near about four months, to get a sugar treatment 'cause I got light bills, burial club . . . . I get a little money and it goes.

Some people treat serious diseases with home remedies. They do so out of habit, certainly; but they are no more able to afford professional treatment now than when the practices began. Those who need medicine the most can afford it the least.

◖ *When they were babies, did either of them have large stomachs?*

No sir. Well, you take that boy. When he was a baby he had a large navel, but he didn't have a large stomach.

You mean stuck way out?

Yeah, a navel you know would stick out way in front of him. Well, a lady gave my wife a remedy; told her to take a fifty-cent piece and bandage it, you know, tie it around him. That's when he was young, and it seems it went back in place.

How old was he then?

He's about eleven months old, I imagine.

Most babies in the black community of Louise are born in the home and are delivered by a midwife with the oc-

casional assistance of a doctor. The number of miscarriages
and infant deaths is startlingly large. (The infant death rate
in 1964 in Humphreys County was 2,941 per 100,000 live
births, compared to the national norm of 1,700.) Recent
medical research indicates that it is during the second
through the twelfth month of a child's infancy that his
death may most characteristically be attributed to the fact
that the nourishment which he received before and after
his birth was insufficient to provide for his growth. When
a woman is undernourished during pregnancy, her baby may
be undernourished at birth. There have been 4 infant deaths
for every 100 live births accounted for.[11]

〔 *All of these children, were they born here at home or
in a hospital?*
    Well, I got three was born in the hospital. The rest
of 'em was born here in this house.
    *The ones born here in the house, were they brought
in by a doctor or a midwife?*
    Well, I used to have trouble, and I needed a doctor's
help.
    Have you ever had any miscarriages?
    I sure is. I've had twenty-six and I've only saved ten.
    This is you?
    And I only saved those with the doctor's help.
    Husband: We lost a lot in one year like that.

〔 *Has your wife ever had any miscarriages?*
    Three.

[11] Of the 690 people covered by the interviews, 107 are women who have
borne children or at one time been pregnant. They have had a total of 607
live births. Of these, 2 were born in a clinic, 60 in a hospital, 16 at home
attended by a doctor, 481 at home attended by a midwife, and 48 under
unspecified conditions. Sixty-one of the women, who have had a total of
311 of the live births, have had a total of 140 miscarriages and 24 children
lost in infancy. On the average, every mother has had 1.31 miscarriages
and lost .22 children in infancy. The fetal death rate is 247 per 1,000
live births. The infant death rate is 39.5 per 1,000 live births. It must
be noted that the 607 births span a large number of years, and presumably health conditions have improved somewhat with the passage
of time.

Has she ever had any babies that didn't live?
Well, we had one that lived about three hours after she was born, then died.
So out of the five pregnancies you got the girl?
We got the girl.

❨ *Where were your children delivered?*
All of mine was in the home.
By a doctor or midwife?
By a midwife.
Have you ever had any miscarriages?
Husband: Many of them.
How many have you had?
About five.

Many women in Louise eat cornstarch when they are pregnant. Some keep the habit and continue to eat as much as they can get after childbirth as a means of filling themselves up. The same is true of baking soda. And the same is true of clay.[12] There was a time when most women in Louise ate clay and starch while they were pregnant. Now, one out of every four eats starch, and one out of every three eats clay. The best clay is said to come from the hill country around Canton or Yazoo City. Farmers passing through will pull off the roads and shovel the dirt into bags for their wives and friends. When a woman cannot get hill clay she may take a bagful out of the side of an irrigation ditch. She lets the clay dry out, or may bake or freeze it, and she will later break off little chunks to suck. Sometimes you can see a woman at work in the fields after mealtime pick a piece of dirt off the ground and pop it into her mouth.

At the hospital in Belzoni, there are beds for one out of every 534 people in the county. In Humphreys County, there are five doctors, one for every 3,740 people. There are two dentists, one for every 9,350 people. There are four nurses,

[12] Of the 77 women interviewed, 20 ate starch "at least during pregnancy," and of 76 interviewed, 25 ate clay.

one for every 4,675 people. Where the poverty of the people is so great, their health so poor, their ability to afford medical care so hampered, and the availability of medical services so limited, there is a crying need for public health programs. The Mississippi State Board of Health does not have the budget or the manpower to provide fully all of its designated services. For the eighteen counties in the Delta, there are only ten medical directors, i.e., doctors, for the county health departments. One doctor serves as the director for six separate health departments, and one of these serves two counties. The director of the Humphreys County Health Department also directs the Yazoo County department. The Humphreys County department is staffed by two nurses and a sanitarian. In the areas that most directly benefit the poor, maternity and infant care and immunization against communicable diseases, much has yet to be done. It is estimated that 35 per cent (more than twice the national average) of the children in Mississippi from one day to nine years of age have not received basic immunizations, i.e., polio, diphtheria, smallpox, and typhoid fever. It can be inferred that the percentage is quite high in Humphreys County. One problem is that in Mississippi, where for ten years there has been no compulsory school attendance law, many children, especially those of poor families, miss getting their shots because they either do not attend school at all, or attend it very irregularly. Shots are given to all children in the Head Start centers.

❨ *Have any of your children been to see a doctor?*
    I know those she [a sister] left are going to have to go. They needs a check-up. . . . See she had tuberculosis and she left here about two weeks ago, and they was comin' around to check the kids, but they got on the wrong road.
    In other words, they been lookin' for us, but they got throwed off and didn't find here. It was the Public Health Department that was lookin' for 'em, but they didn't find this place.

Maternity and child care services in Humphreys County barely exist. None of the people talked with in Louise could recall ever having heard of any lectures or courses being offered in child care. When medical problems arise during pregnancy or during a child's infancy that force a mother to go to the health department in Belzoni, she will be referred to a private physician for treatment that she often cannot afford. The department supervises 14 "granny" midwives in the county. Many mothers are assisted in their delivery by women who call themselves "midwives" but are under no supervision from the county. There are no nurse-midwives in the county.

What is desperately lacking in Humphreys County is free or inexpensive medical help and enough dentists, free or inexpensive hospital care and enough hospital beds, and free medicine. There are at this time no programs, federal or state, operating in the county aimed at fulfilling these needs.

VI The Disintegration of the Black Community

The community of the poor in Louise was built around the plantation. Plantation life was both secure and terrible. To ease the painful, and to maintain and strengthen the bonds of community, the people had their churches, their weekend gathering spots, and their schools. That these institutions were able to sustain the spirit, and, in a fashion, the economy of the poor community when conditions on the plantation were at their best, is in itself a miracle. But now the security provided by the plantation system has collapsed. Neither the old institutions themselves nor the forces created by them are capable of handling the overwhelming social, political, and economic problems faced by the poor of Louise today. The following is a description of the part that these several forces have played in holding together the poor community in the past and why there cannot now grow from the primary institutions, the church and the schools, the true leadership needed to build a new framework to replace that of the plantation.

THE CHURCH

It has been said that services at the small country backwoods churches provided for the black poor a release for the pressures that must build up in men living in continual poverty and subjected to constant racial slander. The emotional outpourings, from whatever sources they flow, of congregations at church services around Louise are certainly dramatic, exciting, and exhausting. Three Sundays out of four, at any given church, only the children will meet in the morning for their lesson, and, in a few churches, the older folks will gather in the evening to sing and pray with the deacons. The fourth Sunday, though, is "pastoral day." It is the day that the traveling preachers, hailing from Belzoni or Vicksburg but spreading the word to congregations a hundred miles apart, complete their circuits and return again to hold services.

In and around Louise there are a dozen little churches, calling themselves New Hope, Big Mount Zion, Love Feast, and other biblically inspired names, and every Sunday there will be a pastoral day at one of them. The considerable anticipation that precedes a preacher's visit turns the fourth Sunday into a true holiday, and it is perhaps so as not to mar the pleasure of the occasion that few members of a congregation will give in to temptation and attend pastoral day services at another church mid-month. Also, most congregations have considerable pride in their preachers. Where religious excitement is so real to a people, and feeling the touch of the Master's hand is an accepted phenomenon, the preacher has a clear role—that of bringing God to the people and raising the spirits of the congregation to a pitch where they may see God—and it is according to his ability to perform this duty that he maintains his reputation and holds the devotion of congregations. During the long hours of each service, the preacher will slowly spin out his story as the faithful get the spirit in them and shout and moan and dance, struggling with each other and with the passion inside them. When the right pitch is reached, when the sorrows and ecstasy of the folk have poured out, then the preacher will end his tale. The church, alone in a cotton field and miles from the highway, will have sheltered a spectacular resurgence of the spirit of the people.

The church has played a singular role within the black community. It is quite certainly the single most important institution. It is the center for community news and information, which means that it has served as a place where political issues can be debated and community policy decided. The church has been the medium through which civil rights workers have stated their intentions, and it remains the place where the most people can be reached the most quickly. Things can be accomplished very rapidly with the church's blessings, and only with difficulty with the church's opposition.

It has been rare for preachers to take definite stands against changes in the status quo, but it has been equally rare for preachers to rise up and fight to improve the lot of their people. For the most part, they have remained neutral and disinterested in times of political or civil rights turmoil unless personally attacked for their inaction. It has been the deacons of the church, elected by the congregation, who have formed the worldly or political arm of the black church. They have in the past taken active stands in civil rights, offering the use of the church building for community meetings,

working to organize their communities, and, in a very real
sense, often providing the elected leadership of the black
community.

Because its deacons are responsive to the wishes of the
congregation and because the church holds the allegiance
of so many, it should now be playing a principal part in
striving to create a unified black community out of the
fragments left by the demise of the plantation system, and
it should be speaking for and helping the poor who make
up each congregation. The black churches of Louise have
shown themselves to be immobilized on all social, economic,
or political issues. Part of the problem is that over the last
several years their congregations have been changing and
getting smaller. Pastoral services would once have lasted
throughout the afternoon, and there would have been a
prayer meeting that night and once or twice more during
the week. The Sunday school would have filled a third of
the church, and the congregation would have overflowed the
pews. Now pastoral service is a morning affair; the crowd
is not large enough to sustain it all day long. The Sunday
school class is conducted in a corner of the first few pews,
and the whole congregation can barely fill the rest. The
church organization does not include as many people as it
once did. Nor does it now reach the same people. Once
everyone attended church. Now the congregation is filled
mostly with women and children, the young men having
left and the working men perhaps feeling out of place among
all the wives. This, too, has meant a change in the effective-
ness of the church as a force in shaping community policy.
For where once men could be reached directly through the
church, now only women can be. And where once women
bore the dual role of bringing up the family and working as
long as the men in the fields, and saw themselves as figures
of extraordinary strength with the responsibility of concerning themselves with the public welfare, they now, no longer
being wage earners, have seemed to relinquish to their

men, in a subtle way, the second responsibility of community concern. The transition is far from complete, but, as it does occur, the church, as has sometimes been suggested, becomes less relevant to the lives of the people. It still supports their spirit, but it cannot channel that spirit into matters of this world.

THE CLUBS, JUKE JOINTS, AND SATURDAY NIGHT

Many black men in Louise and Midnight are members of the Masons or Elks. As far as the whole community is concerned, the clubs do very little, but they do allow their members a chance for a little fun once a month and hold dances that draw the youngsters from all over the county. What is important, however, is that their meeting halls, virtually the only large, black-owned buildings in the small towns of the South, have been available for use as a community centers, Head Start centers, and halls for civil rights meetings. In Lousie, one of the two Head Start centers leases the Masons' Hall. In Belzoni, the NAACP holds meetings three times a week in the Taborin Hall of the Elks' club, which at one time also housed a Head Start center.

The clubs, juke joints, or roadhouses have sometimes been as cooperative with their facilities as the fraternal societies. Head Start centers, in crying need of space to handle countless children, have been forced to move into private clubs where every morning the teachers would arrange and decorate the room, and every evening patiently re-package the toys and remove the children's paintings from the walls. The roadside beer and sandwich establishment is perhaps the field most fully exploited by the black entrepreneur. Because men like a place to eat their lunches and gather after work, because there has to be some place to go on Friday night, and because these facilities are denied, or not provided in the right style, by white businesses, juke joints have cropped up in the black communities. They swarm with people on weekend nights. Many are men yet dirty from the fields, worn out after a week of heavy work and anxious to mix and relax; such a man wants to remember (as W. J. Cash says of the white southerner) that he's one hell of a fellow. The girls come to dance, the boys to show off, the married couples because it is the only place that they have had to go to for most of their lives, and the old men to watch. Groups of people wander in and out, usually without buying anything. The ladies are dressed in whatever might pass for a party dress. Occasionally, outside amidst the cars jammed together, a fight will get started among the few boys. In Belzoni, the police force claims several Negro officers (with no power to arrest a white man) whose job is to roam the night spots and to keep things quiet. In Louise there is a "colored law" (who lacks the authority to arrest anyone) whose job is to snoop around the roadhouses and dairy bars to find out, for the white folks, what his neighbors are up to.

❲ There's not a colored law in the state of Mississippi that's my friend. If a friend of mine becomes a cop, he's not my friend. If he's a law in Mississippi, I don't know him.

Saturday is payday, and Saturday night is the real farmers' night. The most accurate method of taking a census in a community like Louise would be to make a head count in town on Saturday night. From all the surrounding country, men and women come to "make provisions." Most hardware, clothing, and groceries are bought on Saturday night. It is an occasion more widely recognized than any other. Everyone wears not his age-old Sunday dress, but just the nicest, cleanest clothing he can put together. Young people and children beg or borrow money from their parents so that they can buy something in town, and along the street they can be seen walking slowly, peeping into shop windows, flirting with one another. The old men lean back against the store fronts in their straw chairs, watching the world go by, or make conversation on the street corners, often negotiating over the price of a bottle of sealed or unsealed whiskey. The whites are out too with their slicked-down hair shining from beneath their finest cowboy hats. The planters show off their big new cars and wave and yell at friends and workers as they drive slowly down the street. Everything, and most everyone, is pleasant. Acquaintances are renewed. People that folks were "worried about" show up on Saturday night. It is the night for cashing the check, paying off debts, buying fruit for the children, and getting special things for Sunday dinner. Anything that interests anybody will be widely discussed on sidewalks, and everyone gets an excellent chance to pick up rumors. In the big towns, country boys come in on Saturday to get drunk and make noise. In the little towns, they come to shop, and talk to friends.

The stores stay open until the last man is off the street. After they lock up, Louise is dark and quiet, except for the steady rumble and pounding as cotton is baled at the gin where the tenant hands have been at work since early in the afternoon.

THE SCHOOLS

By all accounts, the quality of education has changed little over the last few years. On the side of the good, however, it is in the schools that first begins that network of friendships and acquaintances which enables everyone in the county to know everyone else. Associations develop here that make it possible for the county to be what the small town cannot—what economists call a market, where goods and services and labor can be peddled and located. Were the towns of Louise and Midnight to burn down one night, the only loss to the major part of the population would be convenience to certain stores. These towns serve as the geographical center of the community, but they are unessential to the economic and social life of the area. What is necessary to these is the knowledge of every man's skills—who is a trustworthy tractor driver, who can make a good quilt—the knowledge of every man's habits—which men get too drunk to work on Monday, where certain white men will be at a certain time of night—the knowledge of each man's situation—who needs help, who will jump at the chance to pick a little cotton—and the knowledge of who are the troublemakers, killers, and bums.

Negro teachers and school administrators have been outrageously reluctant to assume any position of leadership in their communities, or even an interest in the affairs of the families whose children they teach. Holding, like Negro policemen, jobs created by the dual system of government yet being expected to serve their white superiors and not their own community, Negro teachers and principals live in fear of the white establishment.

In Midnight, there is a black elementary school and in Louise a black high school, which had over four times as many pupils as the white school (when the latter existed) but fewer than twice the number of teachers. What teachers there are, however, have probably not registered to vote for fear of jeopardizing their jobs. They, in the natural positions of leadership that fall to the teacher and professional, have consistently resisted all pleas to involve themselves in the struggles of their community. Of course, across the South there have been many exceptions to the general apathy of the public school personnel. Many college professors and administrators, and some high school teachers, have worked hard on behalf of civil rights. Some county school systems in the South have released schools for summer Head Start centers at the insistence of black principals. Some public school teachers have worked with children in OEO[13] day care centers. In Humphreys County, a teacher sits on the county committee of the Friends of the Children of Mississippi (FCM) Head Start system. Still, the involvement of teachers in community action has been even less than that of the preachers, who can point to members or prospective members of their ranks in the Southern Christian Leadership Conference, the Student Non-Violent Coordinating Committee, and Congress of Racial Equality of the early 1960s, and in local groups like the Delta Ministry[14] (a project of the National Council of Churches), located in Washington County (Greenville) which borders on Humphreys County. The teachers, hamstrung by being employees of the county and set apart by their complicity in a disgraceful and unconstitutional educational system, have themselves withdrawn and forgotten the needs of their people.

It has thus become clear that no new arrangement of community development will spring from the old leadership of the black community, the churches and the schools. It can also be seen that the institutions and routines that were built around the plantation system will not now be useful in creating something which will sustain those people who have been displaced from the plantation as it undergoes its transition toward modern efficiency. The last years of civil rights turmoil have brought great hope to the black men in Mississippi. In Louise there has been developed a new program, Head Start, which was not born of the plantation system, and which has drawn for its local leadership upon a too-long-neglected source—the independent black small farmer.

[13] The Office of Economic Opportunity; called by some: The War on Poverty.
[14] The Delta Ministry does research, gives out clothes, sets up conferences, and supports community projects.

VII   Civil Rights and Community Organizations

Louise and Midnight were passed over, as were many little towns, by the civil rights activity in the Delta in 1963 and 1964. Belzoni was not:

❨ When it first started, COFO [Council of Federated Organizations] came here and set up a voter registration drive. That lasted about a year. After that we organized the NAACP. We organized the NAACP in 1967, and that was when the biggest push in the civil rights movement came in Humphreys County. We've put on quite an effective boycott against the stores and brought suits against the schools, in fact against the whole county . . . . Reverend Lee was killed back in '55 and Gus Courts was shot . . . . I believe he was shot for pushin' for the right to vote . . . . They had some kind of autopsy on Reverend Lee and they found the pellets in his jaw, shotgun pellets, but they said it was dental fillings so that was as far as it went . . . . They [Sunflower and Sharkey Counties] had more activity in them than Humphreys County has . . . .

Has anything been done in Louise and Midnight?

No, not yet. Some people in Louise joined the NAACP, but no one down there is really active. So Louise sort of stands off by itself. The people are kind of scared of what might happen. [Willie Hazelwood, Director of the NAACP, Humphreys County.]

A few men and women in Louise harbored civil rights workers from Sharkey County and became active in the precinct affairs of that county's Mississippi Freedom Democratic Party (MFDP), but it was not until 1966, when one column of the Meredith March Against Fear came proudly down U.S. 49 through Belzoni, through Midnight, through Louise, that the people first began going in numbers to the courthouse to register to vote. One man tells it this way:

❮ The Meredith March came right down the highway here. There was a long line of them, singing and shouting. People came running out of the fields to see and wave. A lot of them started in marchin'. At school they tried to keep them in, but the kids ran out and got in the line with them and started marchin'. Some of them went all the way to Jackson. Mr. ――― boarded up his drink machines so they couldn't buy a pop. In Louise all of the stores closed. There wasn't a white man in them streets . . . . A lot of us registered behind the Meredith March. I did. A whole lot of people did.

The boycott effort in Belzoni has united the black community there in a way that nothing else ever has, but it has yet done little to Louise and Midnight. The Negro police officer in Louise was added to the force primarily because the white merchants wanted a way to learn about and to stop any attempts at spreading the boycott to those little towns. The state of political organization in Louise, however, is not what it is in Belzoni. There are perhaps fifteen members of the NAACP in Louise and not all of these attend meetings in Belzoni or in Sharkey County.

Louise has two precious Head Start centers. The confusing and sorry history of the CDGM, MAP (Mississippi Action for Progress), FCM conflict is well illustrated by the battle in Humphreys County. In 1965 the Child Development Group of Mississippi (CDGM) was funded by OEO to administer Head Start centers in twenty-two counties, including Humphreys. Two centers were set up in Belzoni. CDGM's concept of how a preschool center should be run was novel at that time. It felt that the people who best knew how to care for children were mothers of children, and almost all of its centers across the state were

staffed by poor, previously unemployed women, trained by
CDGM in the techniques of bringing words, music, colors,
and sounds alive in the minds of three-to-five-year-olds. In
this way, poor women who had never in their lives earned
more than three dollars a day chopping cotton were given
the opportunity to earn a decent salary. It was, and remains, an outrage in the white establishment's view of
things that money it does not control is placed in the hands
of black people. In October, 1966, OEO bowed to pressures, charged CDGM with mishandling of funds, and
terminated the grant. But the centers in Humphreys
County and in several other counties did not close down.
In buildings offered free by their black owners and by
churches, women worked without pay to see that the
children, even if they could no longer regularly get a hot
meal at the center, got loving attention each day. To raise
funds for the approximately seventy-five centers operating on
a volunteer basis, Friends of the Children of Mississippi
was established.

To fill the void left by CDGM, an organization with
more compromising policies, MAP, was formed and funded
by OEO. In its beginning, MAP was more rigid in determining the qualifications of its personnel, especially for its
county staff, and many women who had been resource
teachers, teacher guides, and center directors with CDGM
found that they could not be hired by MAP, and were
determined to keep working with what, in any case, were
overflowing numbers of children. In January, 1967, CDGM
was refunded, but did not include Humphreys County
which was to be exclusively MAP. The old CDGM centers
in five counties including Humphreys (plus a sixth that
had not been CDGM) refused to be administered by
MAP and organized themselves under the name of Friends
of the Children of Mississippi. Financed, barely, by stop-
gap grants from a foundation and the Board of National
Missions of the United Presbyterian Church, FCM was

able to provide some assistance in keeping the centers going and bringing in a bit of food and clothing for the children. FCM maintained through most of the next year two centers in Belzoni and set up one in Louise. MAP moved into Belzoni in the spring of 1967 where, in competition with FCM, it opened two centers and into Louise where it opened the second Louise center.

For seventeen long months, FCM functioned in what was officially a MAP county. The MAP centers, when they were opened, were well equipped, the children well fed, and the teachers paid. The FCM centers were furnished with handmade toys, the children had no milk, and the teachers had no money. In a final reshuffling, after pleas for a settlement "in the name of the children" from citizens and organizations all over the country, FCM was funded for four of the six counties (including Humphreys) served by both FCM and MAP.

In Louise, the results of the conflict can still be seen. What was at one time the MAP center is a large, well-constructed building, paneled on the inside and filled with new toys, plastic cushions for the children to sleep on, and piles of story books. Three doors away the old FCM center is only now recovering from its year and a half without money. The building is tiny and cramped, the walls are full of cracks, and all last winter the wind blew steadily through the one-room building. The center has three units of seventeen children each that must be accommodated in that space, or in a tiny play area separated from U.S. 49 by a wire fence. The toys are mostly handmade. The children play with tires in the yard. There are barely enough plates to feed all of the children at once. During the last week that I lived in Louise, money was finally allocated to build an extension to the building that will allow for two more units of children. Slowly, a trickle of new books, new equipment, new plates, and new toys is beginning to arrive at the center.

(I'm a county teacher guide for FCM. I work with the teachers and the children. Help train the teachers, and work with the children. We try to get the children interested in things. We let the children pick different alphabets and put them together. We make puzzles. We're trying to teach them themselves. We make puzzles and put them together. We have songs about my eyes, my nose, my mouth. We're trying to get the children acquainted with themselves, and after we get them acquainted with themselves then they'll know—we're trying to let them know—that they're just as important as anybody else. And to really let them know that they are important, they first have to know about themselves.

Head Start has had an especially wonderful effect upon the Louise community. When the first visions of the life-giving power of federal assistance were stolen away, the people, rather than recoiling in bitterness, determined to make good themselves the OEO promise of a place where withdrawn and underfed children could be made to laugh and to play together, and to learn to understand and enjoy the world of people and things: a place run by poor men and women elected in community meetings, a place staffed by poor men and women (carefully selected by the center council), a place where children could eat a hot lunch, and, most important, a place of their own where everything and everybody connected with it would be decent. It has been the first step in community action ever taken in the long history of the black people in that plantation town.

To keep the center going, they used their sparse resources. Near the end, when small salaries were being given out, the center was forced to move into a smaller building. Two units of children were cut; their teachers were left jobless. The remaining teachers divided their salaries so that even those hurt in the cutback received an equal share of what little there was. When OEO finally approved FCM's budget and the center was required to come up to federal standards of adequacy, the people in the community contributed money to seal the walls, to put linoleum over the holes in the floor, and to buy a shield for the gas heater.

The nomination and election of members for the center committee defined which men in Louise would be responsible for the affairs of the community. Almost all of those elected are small farm owners. They have taken their role seriously, and having once been proclaimed leaders will continue to be leaders in whatever concerns their small town.

When FCM first was established in Louise, the white community put up a stiff fight to get rid of it. Tenants were forbidden to work for the center or to drive children there. The welfare checks of the teachers and cooks were threatened and generally cut back, even though FCM could not afford to pay salaries. Women on the plantations were told not to send their children to the "civil rights school." Men were refused employment because their wives worked for Head Start. But all of this, for the most part, has ended. In place of resistance there is nastiness. For example, the town has not moved the "65 MPH" sign on the road out of Louise past the center. Tourists' cars continue to roar by as the children pile out of station wagons that bring them to school. But the larger struggle seems almost won. It has been a meaningful one, intended not so much to prove, as simply not to be deterred from, a belief that the poor best know what's best for the poor.

⟮ It seems that we did more for the county last year, working volunteer, than we did when we were workin' for CDGM, because the reason I say this is that we got a lot of children in school that didn't have birth certificates, we got a lot of children clothes and shoes that hadn't ever been in school, and we found lots of families that was fastened up in the house that people didn't even know was in the county; and we helped a lot of children with doctor care . . . . Some of them would be just lined with sores

and their little stomachs would be pushed out. So I think
FCM has done a wonderful job. We had some little children that when they walked in the door couldn't even
stand up. We worked so long without any money that
really what we were working for was not a salary. There
was one thing that we wanted to prove: that we could do
something if we was allowed a chance. That's why we
worked two years for nothing. We just wanted to prove
that we could do it and do a good job, and we did do a
good job.

There are now in Louise five units of children in Head
Start centers. In all of Humphreys County there are approximately twenty-six units, for a total of 450 children. This is
the maximum number allowed for in the budget. There are
approximately 800 children of poor families between three
and five years of age in the county for whom there is no
room in the centers.

❨ *Could you make a guess as to how much you spend
on food in a month?*
I spend so much. I don't spend no more'n I have. I
spend all of my check, and sometimes I have to go back
and take up debt before the month is out.

VIII Problems with Assistance Programs

WELFARE

While most agencies of the county government, such as
those concerned with roads and agriculture, are controlled
and administered by the planters for the planters, there is

only one agency, excepting the public school system, concerned mainly with the black community, and that is the welfare department. Though in many matters the welfare department abides by standardized regulations and becomes an overly objective bureaucracy, heartless and pitiless, it is frequently used as a tool to manipulate the black man and thus in that aspect becomes too personal. It gives the planter, then, yet another avenue of control over the black and the poor. In Humphreys County, as in the rest of the state, one encounters reports that welfare checks were cut off in the early 1960s as a means of stopping black people from registering to vote. More recently, it is said, early participants and staff members of the Head Start programs in Humphreys County had their checks stopped or reduced to force them out of the project. Head Start center personnel, who received their salaries only in spurts, have seen their welfare checks reduced each time a little money was paid out, and the cuts not restored until long after the money stopped coming. The boards of supervisors in Mississippi, which in the Delta is to say the planters, have no legal authority over the county welfare departments, but do have their considerable influence to wield against them. Those tenants on the supervisors' plantations in Humphreys County having any claim to eligibility receive welfare benefits that seem guaranteed for the elected term of their boss. This guarantee, which acts as an incentive for good work, also serves the planter as an assurance that none of his tenants will cause any trouble.[15]

It should be noted that things are improving. It only rarely happens now that county welfare departments will ignore an explicit rule set down by the state. The right of an

---

[15] In an OEO, HEW, USDA listing of the 255 most needy counties in the nation, Humphreys County ranks 54th. In a recent report by the Citizens' Board of Inquiry into Hunger and Malnutrition, HUNGER, USA, a list of statistics on "hunger counties" showed that 71.5 per cent of the population of Humphreys County were in poverty, but only 12.1 per cent of the poor were on welfare.

applicant to appeal the decision of the county agent to a state board is more widely known and understood. The county, however, controls the speed with which it handles cases; the difference between an application's being approved one month or the next can be the difference between subsistence and acute hunger. A more vital point, and one which will be returned to later, is that while eligibility for welfare and the size of the check are established by a schedule of income set by the state, the county welfare agent has the responsibility for determining an applicant's income. It is very difficult to ascertain the annual income of a tenant farmer who works irregularly and by the hour, and who most likely keeps no records; so the welfare department can set a man's income at almost any point that it likes without being challenged. The agent often gets from the planter his figures for the income of his tenant, which again gives the power over the check back to the planter. The county welfare department also administers either the surplus commodities or food stamp program of the U. S. Department of Agriculture and handles these programs in much the same way, and to the same ends, as it does the welfare checks.

The welfare system, as has often been remarked, has certain built-in shortcomings. Though the federal government contributes the major portion of the welfare budget in Mississippi—83.3 per cent in the case of Aid to Dependent Children (ADC) payments—the state still has too little money to give substantial assistance to welfare recipients. Payments in the categories of Aid to the Permanently and Totally Disabled (APTD), Aid to the Blind (AB), and Old Age Assistance (OAA) are usually $50 a month. Though $600 a year is a very small amount, it is still almost three times as large as the per capita income of the poor people in Louise. Most recipients of APTD and OAA, however, support families with their checks. The amount paid out for Aid to Dependent Children is clearly inadequate for actual child support.

Maximum ADC payments in Mississippi are based roughly on the formula of $25 a month for the first child and $10 a month for each other child under eighteen years of age. The state sets the standard of living scale for families of all sizes, and the above-mentioned maximum payments are approximately 27 per cent of what the state estimates to be a minimal standard of living. But most families cannot claim the maximum allowance. For a mother and three children living on a plantation where their home is provided, the state establishes the living requirements at $125 a month. If the mother earns approximately $72 a month as a maid, the size of her ADC check will be figured on the basis of the $53 that she falls short of the standard. The established payment is $15 a month, about 28 per cent of the difference. Three children are supported on $18 a week from the mother's earnings and $5 a month apiece from the welfare department.

The states with the greatest percentage of poor people, and thus the smallest budgets, are the least capable of providing decent welfare assistance. And, in racially divided Mississippi where the white man runs the welfare department and the poor are predominantly black, the possibility of fair administration of the system, especially on the local level, is quite remote.

(*What do you do?*
I works by the day.
On the plantation?
Yes.
Do you work all year round or are there parts of the year when you don't work?
Well, I chops a little bit, and I picks a little cotton.

Do you work about every day?

No sir, not every day. I make about two or three days a week.

Could you give me an idea of what your income is in a month or a year?

Well, near as I can get at it, about $75 or $80.

A month?

No, I don't make that much a month. I make that much in the run of about two or three months.

Are you getting food stamps?

No. They said I was makin' too much. I couldn't see how I was makin' too much for food stamps.

COMMODITIES AND FOOD STAMPS

The federal government has two main programs to assist low-income families in obtaining adequate amounts of food: direct distribution or surplus commodities, and the food stamp program. The commodity distribution program has existed since 1949. Its purpose is to prevent the waste of agricultural surpluses, created mainly through the price support operations of the USDA, by distributing free the surplus, unmarketable goods to the poor. The basic commodities, cornmeal, corn grits, rice, flour, non-fat dry milk, peanut butter, and rolled wheat, are given out each month in counties that have requested and been approved for the program. From month to month, the basic goods will be supplemented with several of the fifteen other staples purchased by the USDA. People in households receiving federal welfare assistance and all persons deemed to be needy by the local welfare agency are eligible for the program.

In 1964, the food stamp program was begun. It was intended to remedy some of the problems of the commodity program, such as the difficulties and the expense of distributing large quantities of food, the low nutritional level provided by a diet of surplus food, and the burden it placed on poor people who have no ready access to transportation and little storage space in their homes but who had to transport and store a month's supply of food at one time. Also, the program was created as an answer to the complaints of merchants who felt that the free distribution of certain foods hurt their businesses. Under the food stamp program, a person declared eligible by the welfare department will, according to his income and size of his family, pay a set amount each month for food coupons distributed by the welfare department. These coupons are worth a certain amount more than is paid for them and can be used just like cash in the purchase of food at cooperating stores. Thus, the food purchasing power of the poor man is increased, and he may select his own groceries at the store of his choice.

Counties may elect to sponsor either program; no county may have both unless the Secretary of Agriculture declares an emergency. The food stamp program is slowly phasing out the commodity program in counties where it existed, and is beginning to be administered in counties that have never had any food program.

Until August, 1968, Humphreys County used the surplus commodities program. Of the black families in Louise, 89.2 per cent were on the program. The remaining families were generally denied participation because they owned too much land or their income was considered to be too high. One family was denied because they had fixed up their house; another was reported stricken from the rolls because the father had been blacklisted by a planter. Almost 95 per cent of those who got commodities had to buy some food to supplement them. The rest of the families were not able to buy groceries and lived solely on the surplus food. Not everyone ate all the foods that were distributed. Many mothers said that the powdered milk made their children sick, and almost no one used it for anything but cooking. Only a few ate the powdered eggs. Everyone viewed the raisins, only recently distributed, with suspicion because a great many

boxes in the first month's shipment were infested with
bugs. If people had a choice, they would not eat the canned
"luncheon" or "commodity" meat (mostly composed of
pork) which was usually given out. Members of fifty-three
families could not eat it because they had high blood
pressure, and their doctors had warned them against eating
pork. Much of the commodity food was stored away for
use in the winter.

In August, 1968, Humphreys County started the food
stamp program. In setting it up, the county followed guidelines that were designed to clear up some of the difficulties
other areas had encountered, notably: that the poor have
little transportation, that prior indebtedness to stores often
makes it difficult for a poor man to free enough cash to make
an initial purchase of stamps, and that a time lapse between
the end of the commodity program and the beginning of
the food stamp program can be disastrous to poor families.
Stamps are sold twice a month in Louise, and every week-
day in Belzoni. The first month's stamps were half-price.
The transition from one program was made smoothly. However, in Louise, participation in the food programs dropped
by 20.1 per cent.[16] The reasons for this can be seen
by examining several examples of food stamp costs per
month.

The average black family in Louise has about seven members and an income of about $1,538 a year, or $128 a month.
The stamp price to that family every month is $54 for stamps
valued at $98, for a bonus of $44.

The family must each month pay $54 cash for stamps.
This is the amount that the Department of Agriculture feels

[16] Eighty-three of the 93 families interviewed had received surplus commodities when the county participated in the program; only 4 families got
all the food they needed from commodities. When the county adopted
the food stamp program, 9 of the 97 families interviewed were rejected;
67 families had bought the stamps, and 21 did not apply. Only 31 of 47
respondents had purchased the stamps every month, however. The stamps
lasted an average of three weeks.

a family of this size and income would "normally" spend on food. Normally, however, that family had been getting surplus commodities and spending perhaps $20 each month to supplement the free food. The extra cash outlay, even though netting a $44 "bonus," is too much for many families to make, and so they do not buy the stamps.

For two ladies living together, eating nothing but commodities and whatever their neighbors contribute, and *who earn no cash income*, the price in 1967 was $1 for stamps worth $30 (a $29 bonus).

Where are they to get the $1 a month needed to buy stamps? And how are they to eat on $15 a month? Sixty-nine percent of the families in the black community of Louise now get food stamps. Many others heard about how much the stamps might cost and never bothered to apply. One out of every ten who applied was rejected as having too high an income.

The welfare department in Humphreys County has the responsibility for determining each applicant's income, and thus who is eligible for the program and how much each must pay for stamps. Farm workers earn money in spurts and only in certain seasons. There is no standard income for the tenant farmer, skilled or unskilled; there can be great differences in the calculated income of one tenant and another. What this can mean in the cost of stamps can be seen below in two cases taken from this survey.

NUMBER IN FAMILY	MONTHLY INCOME	STAMP PRICE	"BONUS"	VALUE OF STAMPS
8	$210-229	$78	$38	$116
8	130-139	58	48	106

To avoid relying on the applicant's information, the welfare department usually demands of the tenant an affidavit signed by the planter, telling what the employee's income is. No official will question the judgment of a planter concerning his tenants; it is the opinion of many poor people that their bosses state that their income is too high.

The value of stamps that a given family receives fluctuates as their income rises and falls. In the poor community of Louise, however, incomes are so low as to put families at a level of bare subsistence. Everyone needs everything equally badly. It might be wondered why, in setting a stamp value schedule in an assistance program for the destitute, the USDA should determine that families with the same number of mouths to feed should be given different limits on the value of stamps that they may buy.

Though a person may purchase stamps at the beginning and at the end of the month in Louise, and at any time in Belzoni, he must always buy either a whole month's supply or a half-month's supply, and he must buy the same supply every month. It is very difficult for a poor man to amass that amount of cash at one time. He does not earn his money all at once, but irregularly, by the day. Most poor people in Louise have been accustomed, partially because of the commodity program, to buying food only as they need it. If they have developed any normal pattern of expenditures, it certainly does not allow for spending a great amount of cash for anything on any given day. If no money is available until the third week of the month, a man will have to do without stamps altogether for that month or purchase an entire month's supply for the last week.

Some tenants borrow the money for stamps from their bosses and try to pay them back out of their month's wages. On some plantations, it is said, the planter himself will purchase the stamps for his tenants and sell them to his workers as he sees fit. The real problem in Louise arises as work begins to slack off in the winter. Most tenants have absolutely no income in the winter months. There is no provision in the Food Stamp Act for lowering the cost of stamps in areas where the income of most people is seasonal, though this is recommended by the USDA. Even if the prices that the tenant farmers in Louise are charged for stamps are decreased to the minimum, they will probably not be able to afford them. It is likely that most tenant farmers will rely on the planters to pay for the stamps. The food stamp program will then serve to reinforce the old plantation planter-dominated system that the poor must be helped to escape from.

Food stamps, in the amounts now allotted, do not last most people all month. On the average, they carry people in Louise through for about three weeks. The families for whom the stamps do last all month are those who have no choice but to make them last. Everyone must spend his stamps sparingly. Using the stamps, people may, for the first time in years, buy an occasional piece of fresh meat. But people would rather use their food stamps to purchase foods that will go a long way: rice, grits, meal, beans, flour. There is nothing to indicate that more, or even as much, meat is eaten now than when the commodities program gave it away.

⟨ Everything I buy since we got stamps has gone up. I don't know nothin' that the price has stayed the same . . . .
Can you buy more with the stamps now than before with cash?
Well you can't. Cause the prices was down before you started gettin' stamps, and by you gettin' the food cheaper you could buy just as much and maybe more than with the stamps because the food's all gone up. Even the bread, the light bread, a loaf has gone up.

The most striking effect that the food stamp program has had in Louise has been to cause stores to raise their prices for food. The items that have gone up the most are those that were distributed free under the surplus commodities program.

((*Has the price of food gone up since stamps came to the county?*
It sure has.
Has any specific thing gone up?
Not just one thing. It looks to me like everything's gone up.

One example is that eggs one week reached a peak of eighty cents a dozen from a low there in the county of forty cents. The merchants themselves were benefitting from the "bonus" provided by the stamps.

((*Did you happen to notice if the price of food went up after stamps came to the county?*
Yes sir, I sure did. It climbed a good bit up. We talks about it every day . . . . Now this evening—I made $3.10 today picking cotton—I know something in there I'd been payin' about a dollar for, the grocer he told me a dollar nineteen. A bag of smoked sausage. But I'd been payin' a dollar for it, and before the food stamps got here we didn't even pay that. I think we'd been payin' about ninety-five cents. But I paid for it, and on the way home I told the fellow I was drivin' with that pretty soon it'd be $3.15.

In one way or another, people using stamps pay more for food items than people using cash. There were reports of instances in Louise of merchants openly reducing cash register receipts when they learned that their customers were not paying with food stamps. It is reportedly a common practice to tax each item in a string of groceries and then tax the total, when the customers are paying with food stamps. USDA regulations made all this illegal, but they lack any means for enforcement.

The smallest food stamp denomination is fifty cents. Merchants must make change for purchases made with stamps, either with a fifty-cent stamp or with an official "due bill" for the amounts under fifty cents. He cannot make change for stamps in money. Some merchants in Louise refuse to render "due bills." If they owe a customer forty-nine cents in change, they will instruct him to pick up two loaves of bread and a bar of candy. The customer often finds himself buying things he does not need, or when he does not need them. No merchant will give a "due bill" for an amount under ten cents. Pieces of candy and boxes of matches are used for change instead. In fact the price of matches has been raised to two cents for ease in making change. If a customer does receive a "due bill," he must use it later at that same store. The stores in Louise do not price their goods competitively; a merchant is not inclined to price a can of soup three cents lower than others charge, because his customers must spend their stamps in multiples of fifty cents, or are tied to him by "due bills."

Many poor people in Louise, three months after the beginning of the food stamp program, still ate for breakfast and supper the rice and meat that was left over from that distributed through the commodity program. Commodity food formed a large portion of everyone's diet, and supplemented what could be purchased with food stamps. Some people who could not afford stamps still ate nothing but surplus food. It is wrong to replace a program from which everyone benefits with a program, even a better one, from which only some benefit.

In the face of the gradually declining ability of the black community of Louise to make do, the price of food, since the initiation of the food stamp program, has risen sharply and has absorbed much of the "bonus" allotted in the purchase of food stamps. The hardest hit are those who cannot afford to buy food stamps. They are caught in the price squeeze that stamps have created; yet they are too poor to buy them and benefit from the "bonus" that they provide. Those who need food the most pay the highest price for it.

IX Conclusions

Over the next ten or fifteen years, the black community of Louise and of Humphreys County will gradually become more vocal in its opposition to the political and social order reigned over by the wealthy planters; and it can eventually be expected to have the power to control all of the local elected offices. In time, when almost all employees on plantations are skilled, they will quite likely organize themselves and be able to bargain successfully for a living wage. These will be the final results of the dissolution of the old plantation system. They will only come about after all of the hundreds of economically expendable men, women, and children in Louise have died, or moved away; only after all of the young men have gone north; only after many successive years of increasing poverty and worsening conditions. The complete transition will involve many years of the meanest possible existence for people. It will be a horrifying period of wasted humanity.

Until now, it has been possible for most of the poor black people of Louise to make some sort of living. The per capita income of the poor people there is slightly more than $200 a year. There is absolutely no flexibility to the budgets of people living at this level. If someone gets sick, it means that money that should be spent for clothes goes to pay doctor's bills. If someone gets sick and someone's shoes wear out, then money set aside for food is otherwise spent. These things of course do happen, and they require a constant reshuffling of funds that are never quite sufficient to meet the needs. Men must always struggle to find money to handle emergencies as they happen and to provide a buffer against future bills. This is necessary for survival.

It is an extraordinary demonstration of human persever-
ance and creativity that families do manage to survive.
The poor men of Louise have explored every possible
means of earning money with little initial capital. In the
late summer evenings, when work on the plantations has
ended for the day, there will be men in the forests chopping
and sawing down trees to sell as fuel for heaters in the
winter. Some women make dresses, and some make quilts.
Men hire out their trucks to haul water barrels from Louise
to people's homes. A tenant not called to work for a week
on a plantation might spend his time fishing and peddle
his catch to his neighbors. A man who can fix a car can
usually find work to do. Some farmers sell a few vegetables,
and sometimes milk and eggs to neighbors. Others, if
they own machines, hire themselves out to harvest the
crops of other small farmers. There is always a market for
homemade whiskey, and many do their best to exploit it.
Even in a town the size of Louise, there are dozens of little
jobs that men must do—work at service stations, paint
and repair white folks' homes, clean the streets, mind
the stores, and many more—which usually go to white men
but still have been held, at one time or another, by almost
every black in the area.

One reason that everyone knows everyone else in the
county is that, over the years, everyone has worked together. There is a continual flow of labor around the
county, and a very reliable grapevine that spreads news,
hints, and rumors of jobs from Yazoo City to Rolling Fork,
from Holly Bluff to Belzoni, from Anguilla to Isola, from In-
verness to Silver City, and to every working man's home
in Louise. And men's reputations build, so that planters
come looking for combine operators, farmers know where
to find mechanics, and girls preparing for graduation know
where the dressmakers are. The men in Louise call this
job search "scrapping." When things are rough, they have
to scrap up something to do. It would be my guess that

scrapping brings under $100 additional each year to a family, but these are the dollars that make it possible for most to stay alive.

(We don't have no medical care here, or nothin', and I'll tell you, what we scrap up, we've got to try and live. It's either that or sink. The only way we could swim is what little we scrap up. Now I didn't say make a living. I said we do that to try to live—keep from starving. That's what I mean.

Each year it gets harder. The techniques for "making it," which could never do more than supplement farm income, show themselves to be more and more inadequate for supporting a family as the direct income from the plantation decreases.

There is just no real money to be made on the plantations today, and money is necessary now for survival. The vast numbers of the unskilled work a few days scattered throughout the year, and they hold down the incomes of the skilled by draining off countless little jobs and performing them for almost nothing. To make the final resolution of this situation come about sooner and less painfully it will be necessary to draw labor off the farm, make a variety of home industries more profitable, and improve the lot of the small farmer so that he can compete with the plantations.

The government's efforts to end poverty in the Mississippi Delta have been met with a good deal of passive resistance. In the latter part of the 1960s, the U.S. Department of Labor has started running a large project in the Delta, called the Concentrated Employment Program, which coordinates all of the federally-funded and state-managed programs in the area related to basic education, vocational and technical training, and employment. The project has been aimed at approximately 13,000 unemployed in the Delta, of whom it might possibly train and place in full-time jobs considerably fewer than half, and its scope is such that it cannot include the tens of thousands of men and women in the Delta who are very much underemployed.

Several men and women in Louise are taking, through the project, basic education or vocational courses, which, however, promise no jobs. One aspect of the program is a declared effort to re-locate men to industrial areas, hopefully out of the state. Public efforts to encourage migration from Mississippi have not been widely successful.

The one effective government program, Head Start, was withdrawn mainly because it worked. The resulting fight for community-run child care centers brought people together in a way rare and wonderful in isolated towns.

One product of the Friends of the Children of Mississippi struggle and other on-going civil rights efforts in Humphreys County has been the uniting of men in the county who can help to articulate community goals and who can help to devise effective routes for protest as well as economic development programs. This last is of course crucial, for the situation in plantation areas has now reached a point where the entire economic system of the plantation must be replaced for thousands of people. The alternative to replacing that system is to stand by while those thousands go unemployed, underemployed, homeless, and hungry in the Delta, or drift northward to swell the bloated ghettos of our once great cities.

X Profiles of the People

§ The head of the family is a very old widow who at the time of the interview kept three of her grandchildren and now keeps four. They farm 4 of their 72 acres and rent out the rest. The little money from the cotton and her Social Security check bring in $892 to $2,192 each year, depending on the crop. Three of the children have never seen a dentist because the cost is too high.

§ The mother of eight is a tenant but works as a teacher at one of the Head Start centers. Her $77 welfare check was stopped when she began work for FCM even though she had received her salary only three times at the date of the interview. She can no longer afford food stamps because the cost was raised to $82 a month. On the day of the interview she ate pinto beans, cornbread and kool-aid for supper. Their home burned two weeks before the interview, and the house they are now in is bare. The children sleep on the floor. The family income is $1,129 a year.

§ The husband is a tractor driver on a plantation. The wife is a teacher for FCM. One of their seven children has asthma. The children are covered with sores and have regular colds all winter. The family income is $2,008 a year.

§ The husband has been laid off on the plantation. He is unskilled and had been tending the few cows, but they are being sold, and his job is gone. They can no longer buy food stamps. The children sleep four in one bed, three in another. The family income is $1,300 a year.

§ The mother of five—three at home—farms her own 120 acres which she bought twenty-five years ago from her wages as a tenant farmer. The farm, which is supposed to support three families, a total of fourteen people, has lost money for the last four years. The families share the work and the debts. A boarder at the house who has returned after seven years in New York works and contributes some money. Their income is $950 a year.

§ The daughter of the woman above and her five children. She attends an adult education school. Her house is a shell; her walls have no sealing. She has no toilet. Her income from school, APTD, and ADC checks is $1,292 a year.

§ The husband does most of the work on a 120-acre farm to support two of the families mentioned above and his own wife and two children. All that they owned was lost in a fire five years ago, and they have been recovering ever since. His wife is director of a Head Start center. The family income is between $2,400 and $2,900 a year, depending on the crop.

§ The husband drives a tractor on a plantation. They have eight children at home. They cannot buy food stamps because their welfare check was stopped and the cost of stamps simultaneously raised. Their home is in poor shape. Their income is about $1,000.

§ Both husband and wife are too sick to work. They keep two children and four grandchildren. The mother was hospitalized after a heart attack and they owe $180 for her bills. She has raised ten children and had sixteen miscarriages. Their whole house is collapsing; they cook over an open fire. Social Security and ADC checks provide $948 a year.

§ The woman lives with her grandchild. She did not apply for food stamps because she feared the cost. APTD and ADC checks provide $768 a year.

§ The father is a skilled and very needed worker on a plantation. He earns about $50 a week year round. His wife is director of a Head Start center. Their house, like all the others on the plantation, is old and unsound. Total income for the family of eight is $3,580 a year.

§ The husband does hand labor on a small plantation for three dollars a day. He applied for food stamps but was told his income was too high. The day of the interview they ate butterbeans for supper. Income, including Social Security, is between $846 and $976 a year.

§ The family farms their own 80 acres. For supper on the night of the interview they had peas. The father has had a heart attack; the son, for reasons unknown, is often too weak to get out of bed in the morning. He owes $5,500 on farm equipment. From his furnish, ADC, and APTD checks, he makes $1,084 a year.

§ The household is made up of a husband, his wife, their child, and a boarder. They farm their own 40 acres, thus their applications for food stamps and commodities were rejected. The farm has been in debt for five years. Their total income from the furnish is $600 a year.

§ The family farms their own 80 acres. The wife is a driver for FCM. They repaired their house in 1963 and as a result were cut from the commodities program. During the months not covered by the furnish, they get by on what their children in Chicago send them. Their income this year was between $1,300 and $1,900.

§ The father services and installs butane tanks for gas heaters. His wife is a teacher for FCM. They have a relatively nice home for which they pay $25 a month rent. But the windows have no panes; their toilet is outside; and two of the children have to sleep on the floor. The income for the ten people is $3,512 a year.

§ The father works on a plantation. The mother is a Head Start teacher. They own some land which they have rented out. They do not buy food stamps because of the cost. The income for the three people is $1,550 a year.

§ The father is a highly skilled machine operator on a large plantation. The mother has raised six children, had two miscarriages, and lost one child in infancy. She cannot afford medicine for her high blood pressure. Their porch steps have collapsed. Income for the family of eight is $2,924 a year.

§ A mother and three children are supported by a $41-a-month ADC check. She is charged $22 a month for food stamps. The family almost never eats meat, fish, or eggs. For supper they usually eat beans or canned spaghetti. They have no toilet.

§ The mother supports her ten children by working as a maid for three dollars a day. She must pay $16 a month for food stamps and $8 a month for rent. She buys medicine on credit for her blood pressure and diabetes. The income for the family is $936 a year.

§ The husband is too old to do much work on the plantation. His wife works for FCM. Their oldest son is too disabled to work. Their application for ADC was rejected because their income was too high. The mother has raised three children and had five miscarriages. Their income is $1,928 a year.

§ The father does hand labor on the plantation. His wife sews. Their granddaughter and her two children live with them. Income for the family is $700 a year.

§ A mother and her adult daughter. They do whatever work they can find. The daughter will be enrolled in a CEP[17] program this winter. Their neighbors contribute food. Their home sits on the ground and on a slant. Their income is $334 a year.

§ The family of six is supported solely by the father's earnings from the cotton gin in the fall. Their income is $334 a year.

[17] Concentrated Employment Program, a vocational training program of the Labor Department which has as one of its objectives the relocation of poor people to job centers outside of Mississippi.

§ A woman alone, unemployed. She will sometimes cook a meal for a white family and earn a little money. She missed buying food stamps because she had doctor's bills. She eats mostly what her neighbors contribute. Her income might be as high as $260 a year.

§ The father drives a tractor on a plantation. The six children rarely eat meat, fish, or fruit. On the day of the interview, they had mashed potatoes and cornbread. Two children sleep in one bed, four in the other. Their income from farm work is $1,632 a year.

§ The father is a skilled tenant farmer. He is paid a straight time salary of $35 a month and $9 per day worked. On the day of the interview, the family ate three meals: sausage for breakfast, dry beans for dinner, dry beans for supper. None of the ten in the family has ever seen a dentist. Their income is $1,635 a year.

§ The father is a tractor driver and supports his wife, twelve children, and a grandchild. The mother eats clay and starch to satisfy her appetite. One child was born with diabetes; another now has intestinal worms; another is blind and retarded; one died when he was four months old. The mother has had five miscarriages. Including an APTD check, the income for the fifteen is $2,992 a year.

§ The father is a skilled tenant farmer. His seven-year-old son cannot enter school because he has no birth certificate. The family does not get food stamps because of their expense. There are two rooms—a bedroom and kitchen—for the eight in the family. Their income is $1,920 a year.

§ The father works straight time on a plantation for $35 a week. He works about eighty hours a week, six months a year, twenty hours a week thereafter. He was hurt on the job and could not buy food stamps one month. His eight children can never buy lunches at school in the winter;

they all have colds all winter. Their house offers barely any shelter against the elements. Their income is $1,820 a year.

§ The household is made up of a twenty-three-year-old-woman and her two children. The mother is unemployed. She pays six dollars a month for stamps; after they run out, the family lives on beans. They cannot afford wood to burn in their heater. They get a $25-a-month ADC check.

§ The father is an unskilled tenant farmer. The mother is a cook at the Head Start center. They have raised seventeen children. The father has not seen a doctor since 1942. Total income for the family of eight is $900 a year.

§ The father drives a tractor. The family cannot afford food stamps. For supper on the day of the interview, the thirteen in the family ate beans. The walls of the two bedrooms are not sealed. Rain comes in the roof. The family income is $1,081 a year.

§ The father farms his own 40 acres of land with a furnish from a planter. After the six months covered by the furnish, the family borrows from the planter to stay alive. Total income for the family of four is $480 a year.

§ The father farms his own 80 acres and actually clears money on his land. Because of this, he was rejected for food stamps. He has eight children at home by his second wife, and helps to support four more by his first wife. Only one of the eight has ever seen a dentist. The family income is $2,550 a year.

§ The father drives a tractor; he does not earn enough ($910 a year) to buy food stamps so he prefers the commodities program. Three of his children have had intestinal worms; all have colds in the winter and skin infections in the summer. They eat their meals on the floor. Their toilet is inside because theirs is the old cook's house.

§ The father is a skilled tenant farmer. He did not apply

for food stamps because he feared the cost would be too high. On the day of the interview, the family ate only green peas and rice. Three children sleep in a bed; four sleep on a cot. Total income for the family of eleven is $1,960 a year.

§ The household is made up of an unemployed twenty-three-old woman and her four children. They cannot afford food stamps. They never eat meat, fish, or eggs. They drink about three or four pints of milk a month. None of the five has ever seen a dentist. They own no blankets, no stove, no furniture except a bed and a chair. Their house has no electricity. The ADC check provides $54 a month.

§ Both husband and wife are elderly and unemployed. They left the plantation last year because their home was collapsing and they could not get wood to burn. They get $74 a month from Social Security.

§ The husband is a saw operator at a lumber mill. He was not allowed to get commodities or food stamps. He has just installed a toilet inside his home and he is laying pipes for inside running water. Income for the family of eight is $3,380 a year.

§ The father drives a tractor. The mother works for FCM. Most of their five children have colds all winter and running sores on their bodies in the summer. The family income is $1,780 a year.

§ The father drives a tractor. He can buy food stamps, but they last him only two weeks. The family gets its water one-half mile away at the county barn hydrant. Total income for the family of four is $1,800 a year.

§ The father suffered a stroke and cannot work. The mother is a maid. Their house is made of cinder blocks, but still they are bothered by rats and snakes coming in.

Total income, including ADC and APTD checks, is $2,900 for the family of ten.

§ The father drives a tractor on a plantation and supports a wife and two grandchildren. Rats have eaten holes in the sealing on the walls; the roof leaks. The family income, counting Social Security, is $1,764 a year.

§ The father drives a tractor on a plantation. His eight children do not eat lunch at school in the winter; they taste fruit "every Christmas mostly." Rats have eaten away the paper sealing on his walls. The income for the ten people is $900 a year.

§ The father is old and too disabled to work; the mother is a part-time maid. Their twenty-three-year-old daughter and her three children live with them. The daughter has had two miscarriages and lost one child in infancy. The family income, including welfare, is $1,753.

§ The father drives a tractor and supports his wife and four children and four of his sister's children (their mother died; they were transferred to another sister who developed tuberculosis, were sent to live with him). None of the children ever gets milk to drink, and the five in school never eat lunch. The two-year-old has asthma. The family owns no blankets, few clothes, and almost no shoes. Four children sleep on one bed, two on another, two on the floor. The family has no toilet. Total income for the ten people is $1,514 a year.

§ The father is a skilled tenant farmer. His home is very nice. The eldest of his nine children works also, but does not contribute his earnings to the family; the family was rejected for food stamps because he lives there. The mother has had one miscarriage, and three children died in infancy. The family income, including ADC, is $2,584 a year.

§ An old couple who farm 40 rented acres. Their total income is $440 a year from the furnish and the crop.

§ The family farms their own 100 acres. The price that they pay for food stamps was raised $22 per month when the father began attending an adult education school that pays him $30 a week expenses. They buy almost all of their food on credit. They own almost no clothing and all of the children do not have shoes. They are badly in debt. Income is $1,140 a year for the six people.

§ The father drives a tractor on a plantation. The family could afford food stamps only once. Total income for the five people is $1,170 a year.

§ The household is made up of a mother and her thirteen children, her father and her three brothers. All of the adults do occasional hand labor on the plantation. The two younger brothers and the thirteen children have never seen a doctor. All eighteen sleep in three rooms. The family income is $2,400 a year.

§ The father farms 37 acres of which he rents 17. His oldest child has been crippled for four years for unknown reasons. Total income for the family of seven, counting all checks, is $1,342 a year.

§ The husband owns, and sometimes works at, an auto repair shop. He was denied commodities because he owned a car, and he did not apply for food stamps. With him live his wife and an adopted child. He is very old and sick, and buying pain killers takes most of his $360-a-year income.

§ The father drives a tractor on a plantation. The floors of his home are full of holes, and he is bothered by rats. His mother-in-law, living with the family, spends $10 to $12 a month for pills for her high blood pressure. Total income, including all checks, for the family of ten, is $1,612.

§ The husband was driving a tractor on a small plantation for four dollars a day, but he found a better-paying job at a cotton gin, and his family is now being evicted from their home. None of the six children, except for an eleven-year-old girl who has rheumatism, has even seen a doctor or a dentist. Income for the family of eight is $1,860 a year.

§ The family farms a rented 27 acres. The mother also works at an adult school. Her nine children have colds all winter and sores on their bodies all summer. The thirteen-year-old has rheumatic fever. Their floors have holes in them; the sealing on the walls is rotting. Income for the ten is $2,456 a year.

§ The mother works on her father-in-law's farm. She has nine children. With her lives a sixty-three-year-old aunt who keeps the family from getting food stamps because she cannot produce her doctor bills. The children eat on the floor out of pans. Wind blows through the walls; windowpanes are missing. Their income is $2,412 a year.

§ The mother is unemployed and was hospitalized recently with heart trouble. The family almost never has meat, fruit, fish, eggs, or milk. The six children in school never eat lunch. From inside their house you can see the ground below and the sky above. Total income, including ADC, for the seven people, is $732 a year.

§ The family, an elderly couple and usually about three grandchildren, farms their own 180 acres. The mother has raised nine children, and has had five miscarriages. Their income is $600.

§ The father drives machines on a plantation. His wife sharecrops 13 acres. Two of their five children had hernia operations in their second year. They have an inside toilet because their house was built for a white man. The family income is $1,540 a year.

§ Husband and wife are both too old to do much work. They could not get commodities because a planter "black-balled" them. There are large cracks in the walls of their home; there are no panes in the windows. They receive $720 a year from Social Security.

§ The father does hand labor on a plantation. None of his eleven children has ever seen a dentist. They eat from jar tops on the floor. The twelve people are supported by $700 a year from Social Security.

§ The father is too old to work. All eleven children are bothered by sores and continuous colds. The seventeen-year-old girl has asthma. The mother likes to eat clay. Welfare and Social Security checks total $1,540 a year.

§ The mother is unemployed. Two of her nine children work in the summer when school is out; the family will not be able to get food stamps for the next few months because they need to buy shoes. One son has epilepsy. One has asthma. Their present house is in very poor condition. Their old one, a better house, burned down in the spring. The family income, including ADC and APTD, is $2,380 a year.

§ The household is made up of a husband and wife, their three children, and the mother, two brothers and a sister of the wife, and the three children of one of them. The husband does mechanical work in the shop of a plantation. They get their water from a well a quarter mile away. Income for the twelve people is $2,320.

§ The mother is unemployed. She has been hospitalized recently for a bladder operation and she is now recovering. Her seven children get colds in the winter and sores in the summer, and some are sleepy and listless all day. They can no longer buy lunches at school. The family has no toilet; their porch is collapsing. They get $67 a month ADC.

§ The household is made up of two brothers and their wives, ten children, and the mother of one of the wives. One brother works on the plantation; the other attends an adult school. Between them, the two wives have had five miscarriages and lost one child in infancy. The children eat on the floor. Two sleep on the floor. Income for the fifteen is $3,472 a year.

§ The father drives a tractor on a plantation. His twelve children eat their meals on the floor and sleep up to four in each bed. Income for the fourteen people is $2,160 a year.

§ The mother of five attends an adult school. One of her five children has asthma. None of them has even been to see a dentist. None of the walls in the kitchen is sealed. All seven in the family are supported by $1,702 a year.

§ A seventy-three-year-old man alone. He does odd jobs on a friend's farm. The farmer built him a little house to live in. It is sound but has no electricity. He has never been to see a doctor. He receives $50 a month welfare.

§ The household is made up of a mother, her mother, and eight children. The mother does a little hand labor on the plantation. Six of the children have never seen a doctor; seven have never been to see a dentist. Three children sleep with their mother and two with their grandmother. Income is $1,108 a year.

§ The father, sixty years old, does hand labor on a plantation. He has not been able to afford food stamps since the first month. On the day of the interview, the family ate mashed potatoes for breakfast and butterbeans for supper. The oldest of the five children is blind. The father has a bad heart and diabetes but cannot afford to buy medicine. Income for the seven people is $700 a year.

§ The father is a non-tenant machine operator. He was

kicked off a plantation because his wife was a block organizer for a store boycott in another town. He was not allowed to receive commodities and he cannot afford food stamps. He refuses to pay rent for his house until his landlord repairs the porch and the windows. He supports his wife and child on $1,200 a year.

§ The father attends a vocational school; his wife works. Because of the money from school, the family made roughly $6,000 in 1968. He was rejected for commodities and he does not get food stamps because he got tired of responding to the welfare department's inquiries about his income. He is trying to send one of his sons through college.

§ The father is too old to work. He needed doctor's treatment one month and has not been able to afford food stamps since. There are three in the family supported by Social Security and welfare checks totalling $1,104.

§ The father farms 4 of his father's 30 acres; he is furnished by a planter. The family's food stamp allotment lasts them two weeks after which they begin skipping meals. The five children in school are able to buy lunch about once a week. None of the six children has ever seen a dentist. Total income, including a veteran's check, for the family of eight, is $432.

§ The father is a skilled tenant farmer. On the day of the interview, the family ate dry cereal for breakfast and pinto beans for supper. The two children in school can buy lunches most days; their mother will keep them home if she cannot give them the money. She has raised six children, had three miscarriages, and lost two children in infancy. The family income is $1,680 a year.

§ The father works very infrequently on a plantation. He has not purchased food stamps since the first month. The three-year-old child has had worms three times in the last year which parents have gotten rid of by spreading turpentine on her stomach. The family has no toilet. Their income is $900 a year.

§ The father drives a tractor on a plantation. His seven children in school almost never eat a lunch. He usually cannot buy food stamps. His two children eligible for Head Start were not enrolled because they did not have enough clothes at the time. Total income for the family of twelve is $1,260 a year.

§ The household is made up of a father, his working son, his daughter and her five children, and a younger son. The father is not skilled in the operation of any farm machines and lives on a plantation that relies solely on machine work. His son supports them. None of the six children has ever seen a dentist. "Wind comes through the whole house." Income for the nine people is $1,690 a year.

§ The mother is a maid. Her two eldest sons found two week's work this summer. One son sends a little money from Chicago. Including a Social Security check, income is $1,380 a year.

§ The father is a skilled plantation worker. His sixteen-year-old daughter has asthma. The mother has raised six children, had two miscarriages, and lost one child to disease at eight years of age. Income for the four is $832 a year.

§ The mother of three is too old to farm her 120 acres of land and has rented it out. Because the family owned the land, they could not get commodities, and though the husband died last year, they could not get stamps. They eat meat once a week; they never eat fish, fruit, or eggs. The family has no toilet. The four people live on $2,240 a year.

§ A mother and her adult daughter. The daughter is a driver for one Head Start center. They could not get commodities because their income from sharecropping was too high; they cannot get stamps because the FCM salary is too high. The two women have raised a total of six children and had a total of eleven miscarriages. Including Social Security, their income is $2,642 a year.

§ The family sharecrops 6 acres. Including all checks, they make an average of $108 a month out of which they must pay $50 for food stamps. There are five children in the household.

§ The husband and wife are too old to work. The mother has never birthed any live children, but they have raised several "sets" of other people's. They are now raising two. The husband is quite ill; the wife suspects he has cancer. From Social Security and welfare, they get $1,795 a year.

§ The father drives a tractor. The mother has a bad heart and diabetes. One of their four children has rheumatism. There are no screens for the windows. Total income for the six people is $1,930 a year.

§ The mother of three is unemployed. Food stamps do not last the family but two or three weeks and after that they do not eat much but bread and syrup. They are supported by an ADC check—$43 a month.

§ The father is a machine operator on a plantation. The house is in extremely poor condition. The cracks in the walls are very large. Including all checks, the income of the four people is $2,810 a year.

§ Husband and wife farm 17 acres of rented land. Because they had land, they were rejected for commodities and OAA. Usually neither can afford the medicine needed for heart condition. Social Security provides them with $84 a month.

§ The father works on a plantation and sharecrops 15 acres. The eleven children catch colds all winter. The walls of their house are not sealed. Total income for the family is $775 a year.

§ The household is made up of eight children, their mother, and their grandmother, neither of whom are employed. The mother has recently been in the hospital for heart and kidney ailments, and that expense means that the family will be unable to buy food stamps for some time. One child has asthma. None of the eight children has ever seen a dentist. They eat their meals on the floor. Social Security and ADC provide the ten people with $92 a month.

§ An old couple and their six grandchildren. They cannot afford food stamps. Five of the children have never seen a doctor or a dentist. The wife has high blood pressure but cannot afford medicine. Social Security provides them with $1,668 a year.

§ The sixty-four-year-old father works on a plantation. One of his sons quit school because he did not have decent clothing. Their daughter cannot hear well. The wife has high blood pressure. One of her children died after six years of heart trouble. Total income for the three at home is $1,700 a year.

§ The household is made up of a mother, eight children, and one grandchild. The mother was badly injured doing heavy work on the plantation, and rather than stand for her needed operation, the planter evicted her. Because of her medical bills, she cannot afford food stamps. Two children have quit school to earn money. All must eat from pans on the floor. Neighbors contribute money and food. Their total income, including ADC, is about $1,708 for the ten people.

XI The Will to Survive

The poor people of Louise have virtually nothing; yet their wants, as they articulate them, are quite simple and are things taken for granted by most Americans. They want to work. They want to be able to log enough hours in a week to make a good income. They want to be able to give their children enough food so that they will survive their childhood and grow up to be strong. They want for them something better than a daily fare of bread and molasses. They want a way to keep their children from having intestinal worms, sores on their bodies, colds all winter. They want homes that can be kept warm and dry in the winter and do not have rats in them. They want to be treated with the respect that they have earned by working, all of their lives, as hard and as often as they could. And most of them do not want to leave Mississippi or Louise—their state and their community.

❡ I have a hard way to go along so far as my living affairs. If I could get me a job that was worthwhile to where I could live, where I could school my children, then I could overlook some other few things that's happened. I would love to be able to get my kids clothes, keep 'em in school to where they could get a fair learning. And I would love to live inside my house, too, well, decent. Other outside affairs, the worldly part—it don't bother me so bad. We have a heap of unfair things to go through with. Right now, I wouldn't make any complaints against them. I would like to make my complaints long toward my house and what I would call my wages affairs, what I work for, my earnings, and so I could see to my own family. That's where I stand right now . . . .

Part II

ONCE THE PROMISED LAND

❲ I wouldn't advise none of my children to go into the coal mines . . . . I took one boy in . . . . There wasn't nothin' else he could do here . . . . I said don't go. But he said I've got to work . . . . I told him not to go and I'll tell the next boy not to go. Fer there's nothin' in the coal mines. You get the rock dust. You get the black lung. You work like a slave.

It is not easy to make the shift from the Delta to the Kentucky mountains, for the regions are very different. They are not alike in geography, culture, climate, or custom. But both have been used to further the interests of a nation bent on out-producing all others. And they have been used in a manner contemptuous of the land and the people. The ultimate sign of that contempt is the condition in which the men and women who have made the cotton grow and have brought the coal from the ground must now live.

It is somehow easier to convey a picture of the flat land of the Delta than it is to describe, for the benefit of one who has never seen them, the cramped hilltops of Kentucky. It is also easier to understand the compact world of the Delta than it is to understand the far-flung mountain region, of which East Kentucky is just one part, and which has a history more murky and probably less familiar to the outsider than any other part of this country.

It is not possible to learn about the mountains today by looking at one town or one county, for there is no town or county which is typical of the mountains. While all are tied together and can tell much the same story about the past and the present, the wall of hills which separates the

107

Appalachians from the outside world also cuts off each mountain creek, town, and county from the others. People speak about "the mountains" and about their own community. They do not have much feeling for what is happening in a neighboring county. It becomes necessary, in writing, to switch frequently from the vantage point of one creek or community to one overlooking the entire Kentucky region. The same forces are at work everywhere, but there is no one place where they can all be seen with equal clarity.

As in the Delta, many people in the Kentucky mountains are farmers, of one sort or another, who live away from and around small towns. Few men are steadily employed. But it has been coal, the companies that took it out, its union, and its modern-day production methods, and not racism, that have dominated and shaped life in the mountains.

The mountains of southeastern Kentucky seem a place quite mysterious to the outsider. In the winter, the snowy hills and fields, marked with smoke from the chimneys of occasional homes, are scenes for Christmas cards. In the spring, bright dogwood and red buds burst from every slope. In summertime, green forests, appearing almost virginal, blanket the hills. And in the fall, the splendor of reds and yellows is matched in but a few other places in this land. Throughout the year dawns are cloaked in fog and mist that fills up the fields and valleys and rises gently to the mountain caps. In the night time, the hills are without scattered lights, and they are in silence. Always the mountains seem impenetrable, lacking a geography that is sensible or that is familiar to the outsider. East and West, North and South become muddled. There are no straight lines. Roads and creeks and hilltops follow directions set by natural, not human, plan. The eye travels only so far as the next rising slope. The horizon is above you and near to you. All that is around you speaks of isolation.

The people who inhabit the mountains are a rough

breed who have given of themselves, their customs, culture and remembrances only sparingly, and as needed, to the outside world. Clothes, speech, food, actions, and attitudes hint of times past. The mountaineers are very close to their past and to feelings sprung from a long history. They are an identifiable and in-bred people who have worked hard to maintain themselves as a separate group. To be from East Kentucky means to have shared a life style with thousands of others in a more distinct way than, for example, to be from New York City means to have things in common with eight million others. To be a hillbilly is to be raised in a certain way, to react to things in a certain way, to have certain things going for you and certain things going against you, and to be distinctly different from anyone else in the United States—anyone who is not a hillbilly.

Spanning this beautiful land is an earthen storehouse of slick, black coal. Throughout nineteen counties in south-eastern Kentucky, the coal is everywhere, and so are the evidences of the attempts to extract it: operating and abandoned mines; working tipples, billowing coal dust, and old and crumbling tipples at played out shafts; coal towns where companies crammed together homes for their miners, now crowded and dirty, or abandoned and falling; Mack trucks, speeding along the highway, loaded with twenty or thirty tons of mineral; the blasts from a mountainside excavation where an auger is to be set to drill out the coal; and a barren, eroded, acid-ridden, mountain shelf where a strip mine has been run and the hilltop, now useless, has been left to wash away down the once clear streams of the mountain glory. Out of the mountaineers' homes, hidden far up the precious streams, come clouds of black and dusty smoke to foul with coal walls, yards, cars, clothes, and children. Mining, mine accidents, mine problems, mine wages, these are a part of life.

Clay County lies within the mountain coal fields of Kentucky. Here, and in a score of counties like it in the state, can be seen the interplay between the highlands—a barrier against outside influence and a fortress to shelter the unhindered development of a people, the fact of coal, and a severe and stifling poverty that has settled upon the mountaineer largely because of the hills and the coal. It is to explain and summarize one view of the problems known in East Kentucky that the second section of this book was prepared. It is not, as was "The Will To Survive," a survey of conditions in a town or country. It is rather an attempt to provide a perspective on the situation of the poor in the Kentucky mountains from the primary vantage point of a single county.

This second section is not a study. It is an expression of two individuals' thoughts about the problems of the mountains; it is a mutual work between an outsider and a local man, Robert Messer of Clay County. Both share the conviction that the nation has not yet come to terms with what has been done to this region. Mr. Messer has lived in Goose Creek of Clay County for most of his adult life. For about twenty-five years he mined coal. For the last three years he has been trying to organize the poor people of his own and two other communities. All of the dialogue in "Once the Promised Land" consists of words spoken into a tape recorder by Mr. Messer.

No other voices were taped because this was conceived of as a project between two men and because it was felt that it was not just to question, for public ear, men about the condition of their homes, or the state of their health, income, or diet. For most families, home, land, and food are things for which they have struggled, the only things that they can claim as actually gotten by work, a source of bitter pride, and possessions ferociously defended.

Not so in Mississippi where living conditions are caused by a white-dictated plantation system. There men do strive to expose what they have been subjected to for they feel an economic betrayal that needs to be made public. In the

Delta, a rotting house is the boss's house. In Kentucky, the old shack is a family homestead.

Another reason for not extensively taping conversations in Clay County is that mountaineers have no special desire to, and no personal need to, mention publicly what troubles them. In Mississippi it takes an unbelievable degree of bravery to speak out at all, and it was an assertion of courage to state exactly how bad things are in that state. Robert Messer's narrative is that of a man who has lived in poverty and has definite ideas on how the poverty of his region can be combatted. The conversations recorded in Mississippi were in themselves part of a fight of the people against the problems of that area.

"Once the Promised Land" was prepared during 1969 in Goose Creek, Kentucky, under the partial sponsorship of the Appalachian Volunteers, Inc., an organization for which the writer worked for most of that year.

Spreading northward from the Cumberland River the mountains of Kentucky are laden with riches in timber, natural gas, and coal. The first great western frontier, it was settled by free-spirited, renegade indentured servants from Georgia, Virginia, and the Carolinas, who saw the apparent boundlessness but not the value of the resources beneath and around them in the virgin mountain lands that to them offered escape from the ties and the crampedness, and perhaps the settledness, of the old nations and the already founded colonies. The wealth of minerals and forests has been, in this century, discovered and exploited, first by the hand of those who braved the highlands and later by those who came to join the work at the direction of powers largely unseen—the northern businessmen. And while the appetites of a growing industrial America have been met by the energy from these hills, and while some her greatest fortunes have been founded here, the people who live here and who have so contributed to the development of their country, have as their reward poverty in isolation, slums, welfare, social security, unemployment, sickness, rock dust, black lung, soup beans, and food stamps.

The inhabitants of the southern Appalachians, by first matching their savagery with the Indians and overcoming the terrible hardships of pioneering and, later, the horrors of an exceptionally rending Civil War experience, had set down generations-old roots in the land and a claim to a share in whatever good might come from the pains of building a nation by the time that strangers first appeared to buy up the coal. When did it become the idea of the clever men of this country that they could, in fairness, travel to such a place as East Kentucky, bringing with them money and perception enough to see the possibilities of a new national industry founded on the extraction of coal, offer to those who lived there a wage for their labor only high enough to outshadow the return from subsistence farming, and later, themselves much richer, the nation much richer, leave behind a region emptied of its wealth, with a history of unrewarding employment and mine disasters and a future of unending poverty? When did it become their idea that the acumen and profits of a few made right the destroyed lives of many? When did the notion of national interest come to include the ruin of a region?

All that the mountains had to offer America at the turn of this century was its people, a grand pioneering heritage, great high timber forests, and an abundance of coal, locked in hillsides from Alabama and Georgia to Ohio and Pennsylvania. It was the timber and coal that made the mountains important, not to those who lived here but to those who foretold a growing nation. So they came, in the years before the First World War, surveying the hills and buying for real cash dollars, from the astute but unknowing hillbilly— ever ready to take a buck that's being given away, for how else could money paid out for an "X" on an illegible document be viewed—the right to extract the minerals hidden in the earth "sometime in the future." But it was not made clear that the four-foot seams of coal running through a man's mountain would serve, in part, as foundation for some of our largest corporations. It was not understood that the tall poplar and oak hardwood forests, sold freely in the years preceding the Great Depression, were so highly prized in those parts of the country where the building, not the tearing down, was to be done. It certainly was not imagined that the deeding away of one's mineral rights would mean, half a century later, that coal companies would send earth-moving machines to cut great gashes along the mountainsides, allowing tons of earth to pile up and land precariously on the hills above mens' homes, in the enterprise called strip mining, all without necessary compensation.

Eastern Kentucky lies midway in the northeastward sweep of the Appalachian chain. Unlike the majestic Smokies and Blue Ridges of North Carolina and Virginia, the gentle, cleared slopes of Tennessee, and the neatly laid mountains and valleys of West Virginia, the Kentucky hills form a tangled, forbidding system of small mountains so enmeshed that sunlight strikes some spots for no more than a few hours each day. Tightly nestled between the peaks, in the "hollers" where the streams flow downward through the woodlands, are the homes of those who settled here, preferring the privacy of isolation to ample or even sufficient farming land. Between ridges, long strings of flat-topped mountains that, as a chain, are in no way apparent from the ground, are "bottoms," wider areas of level land opening the terrain up to the sky. Here the branches of streams converge to form creeks along which crops can actually be sown.

In East Kentucky, the land is not something to be worked and made productive under man's hand. For the most part it cannot be cultivated; tractors cannot manage the sheer inclines. It is not a land that can be made to work for men as can the fertile South and Midwest. The mountains can be cleared for pasture, and coal can be cut from within them. In the past, men cleaned huge areas of timber; now they strip mine it. But aside from these ventures, which have a dramatic and purely destructive effect upon the land, the mountains have been taken as they were found. They force upon people the impression of a changeless world, and a world full of natural imponderables like the terrible floods of '49 and '59, '63 and '66. These were so unmanageable that creek beds in many places still serve as roads, and in these parts roads, once built, cannot even hopefully be kept in good repair. A world where customs and a timeless religion form laws governing most daily action. One where strangers had seldom set foot and are now met with open suspicion. A world of people very much perplexed by modern America.

Well, I was born in Clay County in 19 an' 11, the twenty-seventh day of March. My daddy was raised in Knox County then and stayed till I was about sixteen years old. Then we moved back to Clay County. And when I didn't work my mother made me go to school, but I had to work. I had another brother and we farmed in the mountains. We tended ten, fifteen acres of corn. We had to work through the summers, an' we had to work in the field, an' we had school merely half a day. An' I had a teacher that when we went to school, we played up an' down the road. We lived by a river, a creek, an' we'd get out an' swim an' play about. The teacher was my neighbor that I'd been raised up with all my life, an' he didn't try to learn us anythin'. And that's the reason I'm in the shape I'm in today. That don't sound very good, I guess, to you, but it's the truth.

I had one good teacher one year. I guess she was a pretty good teacher. She tried to learn us. But we actually hadn't any learnin'. It was very hard to learn, at least with me. You know how boys was. And this boy an' me, we'd do all we wanted to do.

There was a lot more people lived further away than I did. My daddy lived closest to the school. The schoolhouse was on my daddy and mother's land. That was in Knox County.

My daddy he made cross ties, he peddled, he peeled tan bark, and he worked around. He had a team and a wagon, and when I was just that high, a small boy, I drive a team of mules to Fat Lick from Knox County up here by my own self many a day. An' I had to work you see. I had to peddle, an' I had to do everything to help my dad raise his family . . . Now I've got a family an' I've told 'em all about this. You know when I was at home, and I made any money, I give it to my daddy an' mother. My young'uns never did me that way. But I've never asked for that. I've been blessed; I've had a little money, but not much. That's the way I was raised buddy. When they needed a dollar, when I had the money, I come in an' give it to my mommy and daddy. Had to. You had to do that to get by.

What did we peddle? We peddled eggs. You talk about the gov'ner pickin' blackberries, we picked blackberries in the summer an' peddled them. I've helped pick many a lard can full o' blackberries. And we'd take them to Straight Creek, there was plenty of work at that time in Bell County, and we'd peddle chickens; we'd peddle geese, anything. We raised a acre of cane. I've sot many a day at the cane mill with my hands freezin' off. We'd grab the cane a week at the time. A mule an' the cane and a three-roller mill. And we'd sell the molasses, but we didn't bring too much: fifty, seventy-five cents a gallon then. A dollar is about the average price of molasses. That's when I was raised. We made it on the farm. If we had twenty-five dollars in the spring to make out on, we thought we was rich.

Well, when I was fifteen years old, like I tol' you, I worked in the cornfields for people. You know there was a few men had money, and they could hire fellers to help them hoe corn. And when I didn't have to work at home,

I'd help these people hoe corn or anything else they had to do on the farm. They'd hire me everytime they got the chance. I hadn't got no job to make money on. It was a cheap price but then stuff was cheap. I've hoed corn all day for a dollar a day, and seventy-five cents a day, and back down to fifty cents. I've worked for fifty cents a day since I've been married. I didn't have no money. But that was the year I was married, I worked for fifty cents a day, rollin' logs and sawin'.

Well as I got older, I went to work anytime I could get a job. I went to work in the timberwoods, anywheres to make a dollar. I didn't work very much at public work till I got married. I was twenty-two, tweny-three I believe, when I got married.

From fifteen up to twenty-three, oh sure, I worked all the time. On the job at home, we farmed like I told you. You see they was a bunch of us kids at home, I believe it was eight of us, and we all worked. An' if I wasn't workin' at home, I was workin' at somebody else's to get the dollar, dollar an 'a half, or what ever it'd be, an' peddlin' and everythin'. I worked all the time. In the wintertime we didn't work too much. We had the stuff we made out o' the farm. We had winters then; we didn't have them like we do now. I've seen the ice stay froze over the creek, son, for two weeks, three, at a time. An' hard enough thay you could run a wagon over it tendin' mules.

Well, my mother was born in Clay County. It was where her home's at on Mill Creek. We took a notion to leave Knox County by some means, and my daddy, he wanted to come over too. An' we moved over here in Clay County, an' we've lived here ever since. When we first moved to Clay County, we moved up the holler here to Ike's. We rented a house up there, an' we stayed there three or four years. Where my daddy lives now, we built that house. An' we, me an' my brother, he got killed in the war number two, we hauled them logs out for the house. It's a log house, an' we peeled them logs with an ax in the wintertime, an' we built out of poplar logs, except, I guess, some o' the ceilin' an' stuff. Well me an' my brother, an' my daddy too, we hewed them logs in the winter an' built that house. We hewn the bark off with an ax.

Well, me an' Daisy, when we got married, we went to Knox County an' stayed one year. It was up in summer when we got married, an' there was a feller in Knox County, an' him an' his woman that summer had separated, and they had a real garden. An' he wanted to sell it to me. Well I gave him five or ten dollars for that. And we made plenty of stuff. We just stayed there one year when we came back to Clay County. But I got good pay on that money you see. He had about three or four acres of corn plowed up, an' I got it all. An' I jest stayed there that one summer, an' come back to Clay County, an' I've been in Clay County 'bout ever since.

When I came back to Clay County. . . . My grandaddy had a place, an' he died, an' I didn't have to pay any rent at all. I stayed there about four or five years, an' I didn't have to pay no rent on account o' it was ours. Then we bought a little place over in Knox County, at the head of Jeffs Creek, an' I made enough timbers over there, minin' timbers an' pulp wood, to pay fer that place about twice. When I left there, I come here. From then on I went to work in the coal mines. I worked in the coal mines about twenty-five years off an' on. I may have missed two or three years. Harlan County, Bell County, and Clay County.

I The Curse of Coal

At the center of the mountain economy during this century has been coal mining. Untold billions of tons of coal have been removed from the mountain region since 1900. For sixty years coal hoppers have been hauling the resources of Appalachia north to Pittsburgh, south to Birmingham, and east and west to the great industrial centers of the United States. The story of what has been given the mountain people—the coal camps, mine tragedies, and low pay—in exchange for turning out to America the material on which its industry has been built has become a part of union and popular folklore. The wage for a coal loader in 1969 is about thirteen dollars per shift, or maybe eighteen dollars and up in a union mine, and higher for the perhaps five machine operators whose skill it is to excavate a mountain ridge or level a mountaintop for a strip mine.

In most coal mines there are jobs for operators of cutting machines, for men who shoot, or dynamite, the coal, for those who load the coal into the cars inside the mines, for the drivers of the jeeps that pull the coal cars out of the shaft, and for those who man the tipples through which coal is funneled into trucks or rail cars. All of the men working inside the mine spend their day cramped in areas the height of the coal seams: fifty inches would be "big coal," twenty-eight inches would be "little coal." The air is not good: it is filled with dust. For the main body of miners, coal loaders, wages are paid according to the number of tons or the number of cars loaded. Generally in mines without union contracts the rate is about $1.75 per three-ton car. The market price for that coal is around $24.00 in Kentucky, around $100.00 elsewhere. Not only are the wages for this labor extraordinarily low, but there are of course innumerable ways to get hurt in the mines. Landslides and rockfalls have killed and injured many men. Explosions in gaseous deep mines have caused the most horrible industrial disasters in our history. The driver of a "jeep," a long, flat, battery-powered vehicle weighing approximately three tons and sitting about two feet high, might rise too far from the fetal position in which he does his job, and rake his back along the mine top. The cutting machine's cable might snap, wrenching a man's body out of shape. Everyone working within the mines breathes in dust from the rock above and below the coal seam, and dust from the coal itself. Miners almost inevitably are left with some degree of "rock dust" (silicosis) or "black lung" (pneumoconiosis) both of which are deadly pulmonary diseases. It is perhaps the most hazardous occupation in this country. To gain compensation for anything other than hospital bills, e.g., compensation for an injury that is permanently disabling, the worker must, in fact, contest with his employer the degree to which he is hurt. This means that the company will send the claimant to "their" doctors, and he will go to "his" doctors if he can afford them and if he can find them. The case is settled by a board of attorneys appointed by the governor, and the claimant is almost certain to be denied workmen's compensation unless he is represented skillfully by a lawyer, to whom would go 25 or 50 per cent of the miner's settlement.

Clay County lies on the periphery of the Kentucky mountain coal fields. To the north and west begin the foothills that slip down into the bluegrass country. Southward and eastward are the more important mining counties: Bell, where some of the first strip mines were cut; Leslie, where big coal is still found; and Harlan, site of the state's hardest fought union battles and still one of the top producers of coal in Kentucky. Mining in Clay County is now a small industry; only about a dozen sizable operations still survive. The miners of Clay County work mostly in Leslie, but Clay has the rail headings to which all nearby areas must send their coal. There are four major tipples in the county where the coal is sorted from rock, separated, and graded according to size of the blocks, then sent on its way in long strings of rail cars.

All day, along U.S. 421, Clay County's main artery, there is a roar of the flying coal trucks, emblazoned with titles ("Ruth," "The Bomb") like fighter planes, and covered with STP stickers, coal chunks shooting off the overloaded thirty-ton beds as they round the sharp mountain curves, drivers straining to make an unlikely four runs in one day from Leslie County to Manchester, at seven dollars a load. Manchester is Clay's county seat. It is a small town of eighteen hundred residents greatly devoted to the coal business. Its other main interest is the farmer, and there are several feed, hardware, and heavy equipment suppliers. There are only three factories.

Well, I've worked in some good coal mines and I've worked in some bad coal mines. But I'll tell you about a man workin' in the coal mines now. A man has got to know how to take care of hisself workin' in the coal mines. The easiest money I ever made in the coal mines was in Harlan County in about '45, fer we had big coal. An' that's the first time I ever went to work in the coal mines jest about. Way big coal.

Me an' Perry Jackson's worked in places where they had jacks six foot long holdin' it up, and we'd take these two-by-sixes and two-by-tens an' make a cross out o' that to hold it up. An' I've seen jacks on things that the tops'd be so soft that sometimes it'd go up in that. And we'd have to cut that like that.[18]

You know once I walked out on a feller, it was a bad place, and . . .I was afraid of it actually. It was a great big bunch of us one mornin' went in an' looked at it. Well I was afraid of it, an' I come out. An' I had Gib . . . . I took Gib, that was my brother, I took him in, broke him in. An' that mornin' I was afraid of the place actually. I'd been in there and seen a lot of timbers that was a' poppin' an' a' crackin'.

[18] Mechanical jacks, wood planks, timber props, and even long four-foot bolts are used in mine shafts to brace the rock top that is undercut to remove the coal.

We had fellers that had gone on an' looked at it too, an' they said they wouldn't work it. An' the boss come around, I'd already come out of the place, an' he said, "You gonna work that place?" an' I said, "No, I don't think I will, I'm afraid of it." I said, "Buddy that's dangerous in there, man may get killed." An' he said, "No, it's not dangerous." An' I said, "How do you know?" I said, "Both of these other fellers has seed it an' they're afraid of it." I said, "You're a boss, an' you can see through that top jest as far as I can see. Nother thing," I said, "I don't have to work fer you without I want." An' he said, "Now I'll tell you what you do. You go back in there an' clean that place up." He said, "There's no danger in it."

I would o' quit in a minute if it hadn't been fer Gib. He needed the work. An' I said, "All the way I'll ever clean that place up is if you go right back in there an' sit with me. An' if it catches you, you'll go mashed all to heck right with me." He got mad at me 'cause o' these other men. He knowed these other men'd all be fer me. I could quit him right there. He tried to force me. You can't force me to work where I think it's dangerous. In the coal mines you gotta use your own mind.

He 'us a pretty good boss, but he got mad that mornin'. An' I was mad too, I didn't care. An' I said you go back an' sit in there with me till the cut o' coal is cleaned out. Set timbers, I'll go back. An' I said the reason I'm going back is on account o' Gib, not fer me. You had to have some experience to get jobs in the coal mines. An' I told him, "I've got the experience an' I could get a job where Gib couldn't." But I said, "If you'll go back there an' stay till I clean it up, then I'll go back." An' he said OK. An' that's the way I done it. We cleaned that cut up, but it scared me. I'll tell you. He went right back in there with me an' sot till it was cleaned up. I told him if I ever go back, you'll go in an' sit with me, brother. I said, I knowed you'd push a man anywheres.

I've had to run some races. I've had to run a lot o' races to keep it from fallin' on me. I've cleaned up cuts o' coal son, an' the safety poppin' an' breakin' in front of me. That's a big tale, but that's the way it does when you go to robbin'. They won't let you drive in the coal mines unless you got . . . three entries. You've gotta have a air course; you gotta have two ways out. The danger in drivin' a narrow place is a lot of fellers gets killed with big slugs a'fallin'. But I've seen many of a timber break, an' many of a top fall. I've seed 'em fall in. You know I've help drive a mine up maybe a mile, two mile long. An' then we'd pull 'em back. You stand at the back an' pull 'em all back out. It's nothin' dangerous. I mean it's dangerous; you gotta watch. If you don't, you're gonna get it.

Oh God, I worked where it'd fall in an' all on 'em. You get this cut o' coal here, an' you move on to another one an' get it, an' you jest keep on movin'. You get out five or six cuts, an' five or six o' those pillars, it'll every bit fall in back here. I've seed a many of them fall in. I've seen one man get his leg broke, but it wasn't a rock, it'us a jeep. They had jeeps. The feller worked the jeep, he got off the jeep, an' he knocked the brake here an' he hit the starter, an' it kept rollin' an' rolled over that man an' broke his leg. That was a good man.

How much head room? Well I've worked in some fifty-inch coal; you know what that is. I've worked in thirty-two. Why I've worked in twenty-eight-inch coal. An' you know how that is. I've crawled fer as a hundred foot at a time.

In Harlan, that was a union mine. You paid your dues. That was the best money I made. That was durin' the war, an' it was all shift work. It's been all worked out. That was a union mine. You could make a good livin' at that price. I think, we'us gettin' about twelve, fourteen dollars. We'us makin' good money. I boarded up in Harlan. I didn't live there; I boarded up in there.

I worked in Leslie; I worked in Clay some; I worked in

Bell, an' I worked in Harlan County. I went to Detroit a while durin' the war, but I didn't stay too long. A month or two. I didn't like Detroit. It was too cold. I worked there in the wintertime an' it froze me to death buddy, everytime I got out. An' I took one of the awfulest colds. It'us a sight. I'us workin' in a factory where they made war materials. Course I was mostly helpin' unload freight an' stuff off of the railroad cars an' things like that. It'us a big munitions factory.

They never had too much coal work in Knox County. They had some, but not like they had in Clay County. They had a lot o' coal in Clay County, but it's about gone now. They got a lot of coal, but it's small; I couldn't work in it. Anyhow, I've had my part of it. I can get by. I may have to go back to it, I don't know.

I've seed many places I wouldn't work. You know when you get afraid. I've always heard said, in the coal mines, when you get too afraid of a place, you better not work it. I've turned plenty of places down, an' I've seen plenty of men turn places down they wouldn't work in the coal mines. An' they'd jest tell the boss they wouldn't work in. Course the only thing they could do is fire you. I've left cuts o' coal I didn't get. Course that feller was anxious to get that cut. We'd worked it; we'd set out timbers. In the coal mines you've got to take care of yourself. You can't let a boss all the time tell you. A boss might put you under there to get a block o' coal. I've worked enough to know pretty well when it's dangerous.

I quit a mine once. That's been about ten or twelve years ago. We'd drive up a coal mine, an' we'd started back, an' it all fell in. We had one way in. The air course had fell in, an' we had about 102 foot to go with jest one way in. It was beginnin' to fall in all around us, an' poppin' an a' crackin' all the time. Crit, the day before that, was drivin' a jeep, an' there'us enough rock fell on his jeep if it had hit him would have mashed him up. Well we went in there that mornin', an' it looked awful bad. There'us about eight or ten of us. We said, "Boys, let's get out of here: we'll get killed." Well the boss wasn't in there. We, every man of us, loaded in the jeep, an' come back outside.

When we come back out, the boss said, "Boys, what you fellers come back out here fer?" "Well," we said, "we quit." An' he said, "What you quit fer?" We said we was afraid to go in there with one way, afraid that would fall in an' we'd be shut up in there, an' they'd be a time a' gettin' us out if they ever got us out. "Oh," he said, "there's no danger in that." There's about five or six of us. All of us had quit but about three men. Well he talked two or three of them men into goin' back. Well, I pulled my shovel out when I come out. If I tell you I'm gonna quit a thing an' come out, I'm gonna quit. So I quit, an' I don't know, five or six of us. I went an' signed up on the Rockin' Chair money, an' they held us up fer six weeks over quittin' a job, but we drawed it because there wasn't but one way in, an' you can't work a man in the coal mines if there isn't more than one way in. You've gotta have two or three ways out, an' we had one. They knowed that we had them, an' we Rocked.

You know they sent me down, unemployment sent me down below Manchester one day for a job. Well I went down there jest to look at the job, an' when I went down there it'us jest a pony mine. An' the mud, it looked to me, was about six inches deep. Well, I went to the boss, an' I said, "How much you make a day here buddy?" He said, "from two to fifteen dollars." An' I said, "From the looks of it, there's more twos than they is fifteens, ain't it?" He said, "Well, you heard me." An' I said OK. Well, I come back an' tol' the unemployment men, I said, "I don't want that job." An' they said why? An' I said, "I didn't make my money in Clay County in the pony mines, an'" I said, "I'm not takin' it." Well, they helt me up six weeks on the Rockin' Chair money fer refusin' to take that job, which I thought was unfair.

An' I felt that if a man couldn't tell me no better story than from two to fifteen dollars, than I didn't have no business goin' in that mine. In a pony mine they have track, an' they have little steel cars, an' they haul that out with the ponies. They haul that trailer out with the ponies. Yes sir. Drive 'em son. It goes a lot slower. They used to have plenty pony mines in this country. There's a company didn't have too much money. He could get some steel, an' he could get some cars an' haul it out with them ponies. That's the truth buddy.

I've worked in coal mines where we'd have two or three sections of men working. That's what you've gotta have. I've seed eight or ten men in one section, or maybe more than that. You know they have eight, ten or fifteen places. When you go to drivin' entries, you'll have fifty-foot pillars an' you'll have breaks an' all such as that. It's hard fer you to know about that till you've gone in an' seed it. But they can make the money.

You'll have six or eight men loadin' coal. They're worked to death. You need two jeeps fer six or eight men. A lot of places, they have timber men. An' they have men who cover your top. I've worked where we had to have two men to bolt the top. If you had a bad top, they bolt it, an' that holds it up with about thirty-eight, forty-inch bolts. An' they have a shootin' man. Men who cuts coal generally cuts it an' somebody else shoots it. You have to shoot it. It sits there till you shoot it. Then when you shoot it, it all busts up in blocks. Lot of times I've seen 'em go back an' have to shoot it over. You don't shoot it heavy enough, it won't break down. They have several shootin' men, an' the boss.

I've loaded as high as thirty ton o' coal a day. But you've got to do a day's work to load coal like that. It's accordin' to what the minimum wage is right now, how much you

*gotta load. You know, last work I done, if you couldn't
load ten, twelve dollars a day, they couldn't work you. They
had to pay you anyway, an' you had to make it or they
wouldn't keep you too long. They'd get shet of you.*

*I've done shift work, an' I've loaded coal too, an' I could
always pay my way. I never was fired. I could always quit
a job, an' go back to the same place an' get a job. But I
wouldn't want to ever go back to the coal mines. I've made
many of a dollar. I've made twenty dollars a day loadin'
coal. Shamrock Coal Company. Twenty dollars by the car.
I loaded by the car mostly. I have worked for twelve, fifteen
dollars a shift. I have worked for ten. I've made twelve many
a time for Shamrock Coal Company. You know they paid
diff'rent prices 'cordin' to what you done. They paid ten
dollars for some; maybe if you're gonna help run a coal
machine, they pay you twelve or fifteen dollars.*

*Yeah, I have a little rock dust. The Health Department
asked me if I was goin' back to the coal mines, an' I said I
didn't know, I might have to. You see, I take X-rays all
along, an' they said I advise you not to go back. They say
that rock dust won't kill you, but it'll cut your wind off
awful bad. I can tell the diff'rence.*

*Lord have mercy, I've seed men that had it hard. Yeah,
I've seen fellers had it very bad. I know a feller right now,
I don't want to give his name, he sued ——— Coal Company, an' he got a big settlement. Which I was goin' to
do, but it costs a lot o' money. An' I didn't do it, but I
should I guess. If you win the company, you're all right.
If you don't, you're hurtin'. That's the reason I didn't
tackle it. I know one feller I worked with had rock dust, an'
he sued them an' they beat him. An' I know another feller
sued 'em, an' he winned. They tell me if you get it too
bad, it cuts your breath off. I can't tell much diff'rence
right now, but I might in a year or two. The Health Department had a X-ray sittin' on the thing that comes in the
truck. I went down an' took an X-ray, an' I got a notice*

*in a little while to come back an' take it over. They took
skin tests, they took everythin', an' they come out an' said
it was rock dust. They call this here coal dust black lung.
I don't know what they call this other stuff, but it's not
too bad yet.*

The Good Things

For all that can be said about the injustices and dan-
gers of mine work, few miners would willingly change their
occupation. They may flee the lowly wage, but the work is
not thought of badly. The coal industry is part of the mountain way of life. It was the importer of the idea of "the
job" as separate from the farm, and still, in much of
Kentucky, getting a job means going into the mines. For
that reason, it is respected as no other occupation could be.
Mining, for poor Kentuckians, is an understandable and
natural way to make a living. It is what every poor man does
who cannot collect welfare, who will not migrate, and who
prefers the wage to the farm. And coal miners think highly
of themselves. They realize full well that theirs is the
hardest, dirtiest, unhealthiest, and least safe work that a
man can do. There is pride in their talk as they emerge from
the shafts, black with dust from boot to hard hat, and make
their way home. Everyone agrees, "You've got to know
how to watch out for yourself in the mines." But also,
"Mines is cool in the summer and warm in the winter."

After ten or twenty years in the mines, should his lungs or
back force him to quit, a man has a hard time adjusting to
the prospect of changing occupations. Even if he had other
jobs to choose from—which he would not have in most of
mountain Kentucky—he might be inclined to sit back and
rest, feeling that he had fulfilled his obligation to work.
The realization of the grace he has been afforded in staying alive through his working years fills him with the peace
of accomplishment and the urge to enjoy his remaining days

as he pleases. But this is natural, and accepted, for in Kentucky, options being few, a poor man is expected to support his family either by farming all of his life, which is highly difficult, or by loading coal, but only so long as he is able. It is no disgrace, at thirty-five, to quit the labor of twenty years with decaying lungs and say I can no longer work, for to the poor man in the mountains, inability to mine means inability to work. And when a man can no longer work in the mines, he is expected to rest.

I liked it pretty good, buddy. It was when the coal didn't get under thirty-six . . . . You see I'm big an' tall. When the coal was around thirty-six, I liked it good, if the top was good. In the summertime it's very cool, an' in the wintertime it was good. There wasn't no snow nor rain workin', an' we worked every day too. We didn't hardly miss any. I liked the coal mines all right.

UNIONS

The union movement never gained a foothold in Clay County. There has never been a union mine operating in the county, though companies worked in Clay whose mines in other counties were under union contract. At the time of the big union pushes in neighboring counties during the 1920s and 30s, Clay County had not yet had its boom days in coal. In the middle 50s when organizers began talking among the county's miners, the years of "big coal" were almost over—one reason that pro-union sentiment never gained much foothold in Clay. Another is the opposition put up by the operators; but then the opposition in other counties, like Harlan and Bell, had been much stiffer than it ever was in Clay. A third reason might be that by the time the United Mine Workers was well enough established to take on the operators in the lesser coal counties, it was too content of its strength to become truly aggressive again. The contention that the UMW has for the last several years been inattentive to its rank and file was strengthened in the spring of 1969 when 42,000 miners in West Virginia, almost the entire UMW membership in that state, went on strike to force passage of a workmen's compensation bill covering such illnesses as black lung and rock dust. They did this largely without the support and encouragement of the union itself. Much was said about the corruption of the UMW hierarchy during the 1969 fight for the union presidency between William Anthony ("Tony") Boyle, the incumbent, and Joseph A. ("Jock") Yablonski, the first major challenger to the union leadership since the retirement of John L. Lewis. Before he, his wife, and daughter were murdered on January 5, 1970, Yablonski was attempting to get a federal investigation into the activities of the UMW bosses.

Wages in Clay County mines are a good deal—about 30 per cent—below those in union mines. And workers in Clay lack the dubious benefit of a UMW pension upon retirement which, as many union men have found out, is a hard thing for many to get. The word union is, of course, anathema to the coal operators of Clay County; but it also makes the working men uneasy for it means troubles—trouble that at this late date might as well be avoided.

Well that's been about ten or fifteen years ago. They tried to come in here you know. They did some people join, an' they paid them so much a week to try to organize Clay County. But they never did get nowheres. They never did get organized. The operators was agin it. They caused a lot of trouble, was one thing did it. They claimed the reason they couldn't organize . . . . You take haulin' coal from Leslie County; they said they couldn't pay the union price. They didn't have no railroad, an' they couldn't truck that coal far an' pay the union price, is what they said. That's what I was told.

Well, they was afraid, buddy. They didn't want any union. It was in Harlan an' all those places. Why they had guards, I've been told, in Clay County a' watchin' fer the union to come in. If they had come in I guess they would have had a lot of trouble maybe. But they never did come. They wanted the men to work, I guess, without it. An' like I tol' you, they was glad it didn't come like in Harlan. But I didn't work in Harlan then, but I heard lot o' talk that it'us a rough place.

I remember when they first started talkin' about it. There was a lot of people in this country that I've seed they tried . . . you know, they joined the union. An' they'd go around in other places. An' they had them paid. They was tryin' to get them to organize the people, you know. Like they'd give me, the union'd give me, so much a week or somethin' to help 'em organize. An' I know of one feller had to leave Clay County. I was told that now, that that was the reason he left Clay County. I don't know. He left all right. An' I was told that they [mine operators] told him to go, an' he better go. An' he's never been back in Clay County. He got a lot of money off the union to try to organize the people in Clay County, an' he'd a been workin' in the coal mines before he done this. An' he didn't organize nobody. They told him he'd better go, if he didn't he'd be the next feller that was buried. An' I imagine at that time, if he hadn't a left, he would have went, fer there used to be a lot of people in Clay County was afraid. They didn't want nobody to come around that they didn't know. And you know, that's very bad.

AUTOMATION

For twenty-five years, mining has been becoming a more and more mechanized operation. The pony mines where coal cars are hauled from the shafts by ponies are now hard to find. Everywhere, while coal production stays high, men are losing their jobs to machines. The greatest change in conventional mining came with the introduction, three decades ago, of the continuous coal loader, called a Joy, from the Joy Mine Machine Corporation of Pennsylvania. It was not until the 1950s that the Joys began to be used in almost all underground mines in Kentucky, displacing about six human coal loaders per machine.

Two men can run a coal machine. They've got machines now, but I've never seed 'em, they've got coal machines now will cut the coal an' drill it an' everythin'. With two or three men. But two is all ever had to run a coal machine where I worked.

A Joy is a thing that loads coal; it takes men, but it's run by machinery. See that cut out a lot of coal loaders when they got a Joy. A Joy can load all a cut o' coal in fifteen minutes; maybe fifty, sixty, seventy-five ton of coal. It's got big arms. It's run by juice, you know an' it's got a big broad thing in front, an' it jest digs that coal right out. It's got arms will fly over an' jerk that coal right up on that pan, so it's got a pan down there. They got a car that goes with the Joy. They push a car up on the Joy. It's got a big tail piece on it, like a belt on it, an' goes in the car. They drive the car back out.

They been here for years an' years you know. I've knowed of 'em ever since I worked in the coal mines. It's been in Clay County about ten or fifteen years, but they've had 'em always in the union mines. Big coal back in Harlan an' Bell County, they had 'em. First time I ever worked in coal mines they had Joys. They make a lot of noises. They scare you to death. You can't hear. Lot of men gets killed that way. I don't like to work around them. They make so much noise, if a rock falls you can't hear it ner nothin' else.

Automation of a Kentucky mine has few redeeming factors except that it makes more profitable the production of coal. It does not allow men more time for leisure. It does not create new jobs, except for those who run the machines. It does not free men for other labor. What other work can a man do anywhere when he quit the fourth grade at the age of fifteen to work at a semi-skilled job, and stayed at that job for twenty-five years? In Kentucky, he can do nothing, for there are no jobs but coal work for the generally unskilled and illiterate worker. Automation in Kentucky does nothing but create unemployment, and unemployables.

In the last few years a new type of mining has been perfected, an almost totally mechanized operation—strip mining. A strip mine runs on the principle that rather than dig entries in the mountainside and drive underground to clean out a coal seam, it is far quicker and less expensive to remove the earth above the seam, which might include the top of a mountain, and scoop out the exposed coal. Or, another method, to cut a ledge along a mountain ridge revealing the coal seam and ram huge augers—drills as much as seven feet across, that can be extended well over a hundred feet—into the mountainside. The coal pulled back by the spinning augers is fed by an automatic conveyor into waiting trucks. This operation requires three men. The enormous D-9 bulldozers that create a twenty-five-foot-wide terrace out of what once was a steep slope, or remove the mountaintop, take one man to run. The tons of earth and trees that are excavated are pushed over the side; this is the overburden. It is liable, at the first heavy rainfall, to come sliding down the hillside, snapping over the trees in its path.

Bulldozers Level The Mountains

Many conventional mines are opened on land for which only the mineral rights, not the property itself, is owned by the mining companies. Most men do not greatly mind a conventional mine operating on their property because it does not cause excessive damage. But strip mines are another story. They destroy the timber and beauty of a mountain. The run-off from the overburden pollutes the streams and creeks with mud and acid. As the creek banks turn red with mineral deposits, all animal and plant life in the water dies. A strip mine violates the unwritten understanding between mine owner and worker that they are mutually dependent, that everybody needs coal mines. For while a strip mine, like all others, greatly profits the owner and extracts the source of mountain wealth—a state of things accepted as necessarily unalterable in mining communities, it does also what other mines never have—ruins the mountains and the streams, and offers virtually no employment.

Opposition and Broad Form Deed: It is estimated that in Pike, Floyd, Perry, Harlan, Letcher, Knott, and Bell counties, title to the minerals has been separated from title to the general surface over at least 90 per cent of the land on the basis of so-called "broad form" deeds signed for the most part in the first ten years of this century.[19]

This means that the coal from almost every acre of the rich fields of eastern Kentucky does not belong to the actual landowner and that most land can be strip mined without the landowner's permission. It is, of course, astonishing and infuriating to the mountain landowner—who

---

[19] No figures have been compiled to show exactly how much land in Clay County is covered by "broad form" deeds. Since 1958 only 3 per cent of all the acres in eastern Kentucky permitted for stripping have been in Clay County. In 1962, 27 per cent (10 acres) of the land in Clay permitted for stripping was on land where the ownership of the minerals was separate from the ownership of the land. Yet in 1967, all of the land permitted for stripping was on the land for which the minerals and the surface were singly owned. This has meant that, for the most part, Clay County has been spared the conflicts, familiar to some other counties, that arise when a coal company, armed with a sixty-year-old deed giving it ownership of the coal, tries to run a strip mine over the land of an unwilling property owner.

takes so to heart the inviolate nature of property ownership
and who often has only the productivity of his land to stand
between himself and destitution—to consider the possibility that his mountains and timber and streams, and
perhaps even his pastures and his home itself might be
totally destroyed on the basis of a deed signed half a
century before when surface mining of the mechanized
and auger sort was not even conceived of. His opposition
to this legalized plunder has been continuous and at times
powerful.

In 1955 a Knott County man brought a case in the
circuit court challenging the validity of the "broad form"
deed covering the minerals underneath his land, which was
about to be overrun by bulldozers. Circuit Court Judge
Cornett upheld the deed but ruled that coal companies must
pay for damages to the surface land. The case was taken to
the Kentucky Court of Appeals where it was decided that
the owner of the land surface had no claim to damages
caused by the removal of underlying minerals.

In 1967, another Knott County man whose land was in
danger of being stripped challenged the "broad form" deed,
signed in 1905, which covered his ninety acres. That deed,
not dissimilar to most "broad form" deeds, conveyed in
part:

> . . . all the coals, minerals, and mineral products, all the
> oils, gases, all salt minerals and salt water, fire and potters
> clay, all iron and iron ore, all stone and such of the stand-
> ing timber as may be . . . deemed necessary for mining
> purposes . . . , and the exclusive rights of way for any and
> all railroads and ways and pipe lines, telegraph or tele-
> phone lines that may hereafter be located on said property
> by the Grantee . . . together with the rights to enter upon
> said land, use and operate the same and surface thereof,
> and make use of and for this purpose divert water sources
> . . . in any and every manner that may be deemed neces-
> sary or convenient for mining . . . and in the use of said

land and in the surface thereof by the Grantee, its suc-
cessors or assigns shall be free from and is and are hereby
released from liability or claim of damage to the said
grantor, their liens, responsibilities or assigns.

In return for signing this remarkable document, the
then landowner, who likely could not read, was paid three
dollars an acre, which at that time, in the mountains, was
a large sum.

Circuit Court Judge Cornett ruled as he had done in
1956, that the deed was valid, but that the waiver of damages
included in the deed covered only damages done to the surface in accord with the operator's right to use the surface
responsibly to remove the coal, but that the operator did
not have the right to destroy the land and that damages
must be paid to the landowner. The case was taken to the
Kentucky Court of Appeals where, in a 4–3 ruling in 1968,
Judge Cornett's decision concerning payment of damages
was reversed. Arguing that since the payment made in 1905
for mineral rights was often higher than the land value itself at that time—a highly questionable judgment—then the
estate of the minerals was superior to the estate of the
surface. In other words, if to get the coal the land must be
irrevocably damaged, the weight of the law must side with
the owners of the mineral, finally defined as coal and clay
and not simply those minerals which compose the actual
earth.

This was a particularly disastrous decision for the welfare
of Kentucky, and it left thousands of mountain landowners
with no protection under the law for the defense of their
property. Appeals Court Judge Hill, in his dissent, stated,
"I contend first that inasmuch as the parties to the broad
form deeds never contemplated the use of the then unknown method of strip mining and never dreamed of the
cataclysmic destruction of the surface, the Grantee and his
successor in title have no right to remove the coal by strip-

ping methods. Secondly, I contend that if rules of construction are so modified and distorted as to authorize the Grantee to use stripping methods, he should be answerable in damages to the surface owners for just compensation"; and he wondered, "that the court of last resort in the beautiful state of Kentucky would ignore the logic and reasoning of the great majority of other states and lend its approval and encouragement to the diabolical devastation and destruction of a large part of the surface of this fair state without compensation to the owners thereof."

With the repeated refusal of the Kentucky courts to intervene to halt strip mining in the mountains, opposition to this devastation of land has taken other forms. In June of 1967, Jink Ray, a Pike County resident, whose land was about to be stripped, stopped the bulldozers at his property line by standing in their path. He appealed to then Governor Breathitt to revoke the mining company's permit (Puritan Coal) on the grounds that the provisions of the 1966 Strip Mining Law (to be discussed below) prohibited surface mining on his land. His appeal to the courts against an injunction barring him from obstructing the bulldozers was denied. Over two hundred East Kentuckians met with the governor in early July saying they would die trying to protect their land. After the state investigators decided that almost all of Mr. Ray's land could be legally stripped, Governor Breathitt, in an unprecedented move, cancelled Puritan's permit stating as his reason the "strong likelihood of damage" that would exist if the land were stripped. Though this was in itself a victory, retaliation was swift, and three community organizers in Pike County were arrested under the state sedition law, which was subsequently found unconstitutional. Said Robert Holcomb, President of the National Independent Coal Operators Association and the Pike County Chamber of Commerce, about the arrests, "You might say we spearheaded the investigation." As tempers rose on the subject of "outsiders," a Canadian film producer, Hugh O'Conner, was shot and killed in Letcher County while making a film on American life.

In other counties, anti-strip mine groups, generally involved in the vocal and widespread Appalachian Group to Save the Land and the People, tried to mobilize the opposition to surface mining. The organization publicly disassociated itself from violence as a weapon against mine operators. Yet some men did turn the skills they had acquired "shooting coal" in the mines to the disadvantage of the operators. In June, 1967 while Jink Ray was keeping the bulldozers from his land, a $50,000 shovel was dynamited at a Knott County operation. In August of that year, $300,000 worth of equipment was blown up at a Perry County strip. At the end of August, 1968, two months after the Kentucky Court of Appeals had upheld the "broad form deed," bulldozers, shovels, and other equipment, valued at $750,000, were exploded at a Leslie County mine. And in December of 1968, almost $1,000,000 in gear was dynamited at a strip mine in Jellico, Tennessee, on the border of Whitely County, Kentucky. Yet strip mining still continues, apparently unhampered by the courts, by sabotage, by individual resistance, by pleas of landowners and conservationists, by a restrictive state law, or by federal legislation.

Reclamation: There is no doubt that strip mining lays to waste thousands of mountain acres each year. The surface mining industry shares with deep mining the responsibility for having polluted, by drainage of sulfuric acid, almost every mile of East Kentucky streams, leaving them devoid of any significant aquatic life. The tons of rubble and earth that are carved from mountainsides to permit augering are dumped over the hillside, forming the overburden. One effect of this is the pollution, and in some cases, the damming of streams with mud. Richard M. Kirby, in a study for the Conservation Foundation, concluded that, "Like acid drainage, erosion from strip mining operations has significant off-site effects. In the form of sedimentation and flooding, it constitutes, together with the acid problem, total detrimental effect of strip mining on water quality."[20] With heavy rainfall the overburden may drift down the hillside, leaving the entire mountain slope a field of mud and splintered timber. There have been repeated cases of damage done to houses and pastures from strip mine landslides and of homes endangered by floods caused by creeks blocked with brush and rocks brought down from the mountaintops.

As a result of popular indignation over the disastrous effects of strip mining, Kentucky had passed, in 1966, what was then boasted of as the most comprehensive and restrictive strip mine control law in the nation. The main provisions of the law are that in order to receive a permit to disrupt land with a strip mine, the operator has to submit a plan for reclamation and put up bond of from $100 to $500 per acre to ensure that the reclamation statutes are followed, that no stripping is to be allowed on slopes over thirty-three degrees (the average slopes in eastern Kentucky are thirty-one degrees), that vegetation must be planted on the overburden, and that the Division of Reclamation has the authority to fine, deny a permit to, or revoke the permit of any strip mine operator who violates the provisions of the law. Surface mining industry spokesmen voiced the fear before passage of the law that the costs of land restoration demanded by law would cripple strip mining in the mountains.

This did not come about, however. The law has had seemingly little effect on the industry in eastern Kentucky. In 1965, 4,288 acres in eastern Kentucky were permitted for strip mining. In 1967, after the law was in effect, 6,898 acres were laid open to strip mining. Coal companies were

[20] "The Curse of Coal: Policy Issues of Strip Mining in Eastern Kentucky," memorandum of the Conservation Foundation (Washington, D.C., August 1967), p. 12.

approved for 288 strip mine operations in 1965. They received permits for 422 in 1967. Clearly the law did not disturb the expansion of the industry.

Has the law had the effect of forcing the restoration of stripped lands? It should be remembered that the property that Jink Ray defended in 1967 was carefully examined by state investigators and found to be suitable for stripping under that 1966 law. Breathitt's action in revoking the company's permit was the first and only such use of that provision in the law. In July of 1967, a landslide from a strip operation near Harlan kept up for twenty-two hours, covered a section of U.S. 119, two homes, and narrowed the Cumberland River channel from fifty feet to ten feet. In August 1968, boulders from an approved strip mine operation smashed one vacant house in the valley below and careened through the wall of a Knott County family's home. At old mine sites across the state, feeble pine shrubs can be seen, uprooted by erosion, slipping down the overburden; and sod grass, poking through layers of mud, can be found in valleys far below where they were first planted. Little reclamation, meaning making land useful again— much less restoration, making land become as it once was—has occurred.

There are several reasons for this. One is that the state has not been strict in applying the strip mine law. One coal company, Peabody Coal, was granted three forty-five-day extensions without fines by the Reclamation Division, starting in mid-July, 1969, when it was bound by law to have concluded its reclamation efforts. This was done though state investigators had repeatedly reported that company's violations. Also, as Mr. Kirby notes, "Enforcement too is a large problem. Consider, for example, the strip miner with a creek valley under permit. Out of ten miles of proposed bench, a mile could easily lie on slopes steeper than thirty-three degrees, a mile the miner cannot strip only because of a state (or federal) inspector. The inspector earns perhaps $10,000 a year; the mile will bring in (on the average) about $270,000. One can draw one's own conclusion; but it is clear that no government can afford to get in a bidding match for the loyalties of the inspectors."[21]

But the basic problem, so far as reclamation of stripped mountain land goes, is that repair of the land is impossible. Since it is the principle of strip mining that rather than dig underground to cut out the coal, it is cheaper to remove the tons of soil and rock that lie above the seam, the end result of stripping is a gutted mountain with either the entire top pushed over the side or with a ledge, or bench, like a monstrous terrace cut along the mountain ridge. There is no way to replace the earth cut from the hillside, grade it back to a slope, restore the timber and vegetation, or bring back the pollutants that have despoiled the waterways. As was asserted in the 1967 challenge of the "broad form" deed led by a Knott County citizen, "Once the soil is turned upside down by explosives and machinery, the topsoil and timber buried, and the surface covered with a jumble of rocks and acid subsoil in the manner common to hillside strip mining, the land is, for all practical purposes, permanently destroyed."

It can also be said that no real economic use can be found for highlands gutted by strip mines. To demonstrate to the contrary, a few operators have developed "show piece" strip mine excavations where pine trees and even peach orchards have been planted on the bench left behind by the strip. It is sheer nonsense to say that these frail efforts indicate that stripped land can indeed be made productive, that strip mines are necessary as a means to create land for ventures of this sort, that anything can be done to restore the mud-covered slope itself, or that the creation of an orchard on the shelf of a strip mine compensates for

[21] "The Curse of Coal," p. 65.

the enormous waste and destruction of hillsides and streams and the violation of the landowner's claim to property rights.

It is maintained by many citizens of East Kentucky that the 1966 legislation in itself prohibits mountain surface mining. "They point out that the law calls for: '*all measures* . . . to eliminate property damage to members of the public, their real and personal property, public roads, streams, and all other public property from soil erosion, falling stones and overburden, water pollution and hazards dangerous to life and property,' and authorizes the Commission to 'require any measure whatsoever to accomplish the purpose of this chapter.' Certainly the plain purpose of the chapter is to prevent damage of the sort described, by any means necessary."[22]

It is clear to anyone who has witnessed the carnage left behind by a strip mine that the operation, by its nature, falls into conflict with this mandate of the legislature. And it is clear that the stripping of mountain land is one of the most inexcusable endeavors of modern industry and nothing less than a rape of the beauty, the bountifulness, and the productivity of the earth.

At the head of Goose Creek, in Clay County, is the Mountain Clay Coal Company, Strip and Auger Mine. It has been operating for about three years, following two seams of coal through two ridges over a distance of more than three miles. At one point, the top of a small outcrop ridge had to be cut clean away to get the coal. The ledge of the strip is used as a road by the trucks hauling coal the twenty miles into Manchester. It forms a better road than the state-maintained blacktop that the mine road leads off of. In accordance with the state law, Mountain Clay Coal Company hydraulically seeded all of the overburden resulting from their strip, but their efforts were not very effective.

22 "The Curse of Coal," p. 42.

Well a strip mine . . . . They tear the whole top of the mountain off, an' they auger it, is all I can describe it. An,' I don't like it. Destroys all the timber, the water, it damages it, an' everythin' else. You've seed it, an' it's a bad thing.

Well, it's not hurt the water up here . . . but a lot of places. . . . You know coal's got sulfer in it, an' it kills the fish an' dries, 'cording to how it is, dries up your wells an' everythin' else. Now this strip mine up here, it's so high up I don't think it'll ever come down here on anythin'. You know, there could come a slip up here an' it could destroy everythin'. You see all that dirt's been pushed over the hill up there, where they tore everything up, that could come off that mountain, if a big flood came, an' damage a lot o' people up in that holler.

I never did work around strip mines. You got bulldozers an' you got these shovels. It don't take as a many men. It's all machinery work. It's not like coal mines. I imagine they pay high. I don't know what they pay. Anytime you run machinery, you get more money. If you run a coal machine they pay you more than anythin' else. Pay you fifteen, eighteen dollars a day on a coal machine, but I expect never to work around another. Jesus Christ, that there's hard work, buddy. An' the man that does that, you eat coal dust all day long. It's bad.

When first people came to Kentucky, they survived as most Americans did then by scratching enough out of their land to feed their families. But when other areas began to develop cash crops, East Kentucky was faced with the fact that there is not sufficient land to grow much of anything in the mountains. For a time, a great deal of livestock was raised, but the South and Midwest better supplied that market. When the coal industry began to spread, many young men quit the farm and began to draw the first regular paychecks of their lives. As that industry now begins to mechanize fully, many disabled and unemployed miners have nothing to do but try and cultivate their small plots of ground to feed their families. As employment in the industry withers, the young head for the cities. Poor communities in the mountains are filled largely with old men, injured men, their wives, and their children. The work in the automobile plants of Detroit and Atlanta is done by young whites from the mountains as well as young blacks from the Deep South. Here in Kentucky is another tragic example of what dependence on one industry can do. Here live people that supplied the coal the nation burned, and who now have to borrow money to buy coal to heat their homes in winter. Here miners and miners' sons stand in line to buy food stamps. What will the mountains get in exchange for their coal; the poor for their contribution to the nation; the mountaineer for his loss of dignity?

Talk about poor people, well I don't know. I don't know if I'm actually right, but what I think makes poor people poor is they was born poor, I guess, an' they stayed poor all their lives. An' the cause o' that is they was raised up in the head o' these hollers, an' they didn't have no money to get started to make money with. An' a lot of 'em's on welfare, an' the welfare jest draws . . . they jest give 'em enough money on the welfare to barely live. They can't get ahead or nothin'. They jest stay poor. That's the way I see it. A lot of people I know don't have a garden. An' until they get somethin' to make somethin' with, they don't have no land, an' they stay poor. I don't know if that's right or not, but that's the only way I see. If they set you down up in the head of one of these hollers here, you jest have enough income to live on, an' it takes money to make money with, an' if you don't have it, you can't make it.

II   Poor People and a Great Invention: The Poverty War

Clay County stands in the middle of the Daniel Boone National Forest, a monument to the long forgotten days of the frontier. Ranked by median family income, it is the fifty-ninth poorest county in the United States. Flung out from Manchester, back in the hills, are dozens of small communities, generally found along, and named for, major creeks where the land spreads out a bit. Each little settlement is different from the others. Three, out of many, are Granny's Branch, Mud Lick, and Goose Creek.

THREE COMMUNITIES: A SKETCH OF CONDITIONS

Granny's Branch shelters a collection of about forty homes crammed together along a mile and a half of creek. There is no land to cultivate, except at the mouth of the creek, and the people living there have a rather nice garden. What brought so many people together on a piece of land that would support so few is a mystery. Perhaps they were lured from further back in the hill by early-day jobs in Manchester, which is six miles away along U.S. 421. Most of the families living there now are related to each other by marriages, and the accumulated homes of each generation leave barely any open space in the community. Some young couples build small two-room shacks in parents' back yards to which they return after each unsuccessful foray for jobs in the cities. The houses are pressed so tightly together in some spots that twenty feet does not stand between them. To find space to build, men have had to dig out and level places along the hillside. This is rural poverty at its worst. People with no land to grow food on must find jobs, and there are no jobs to be had. Children born into such communities have no base to strike out from. There is no money to clothe them for school; there is no money to carry them north to look for paying work. Probably half the families on the branch draw welfare. The rest have no money coming in or live by occasional jobs in the mines or in town. Even for the thrifty parent, welfare provides barely enough to feed and clothe a family. The children—who are faced with rising up out of a poverty that offers no chances—are the ones most damaged by living in a community of landless welfare recipients. Others, the sons of poor farmers, can at least scratch together a little spending money working in their neighbors' gardens. Clay County has done little to change the state of things in Granny's Branch. In fact it seems to have balked, in every possible way, at improving the lot of the community. Not until 1969 was a road begun along the creek. Until that time, cars and children, hiking out to the highway to go to school, had to negotiate the only open passageway, the creek itself.

The community of Mud Lick or Sand Hill, sits atop a high and very beautiful pine-covered mountain in the backwoods of Clay County. Geographically, it is about the most isolated community of its size, about forty-five families, in the county, and recent improvements in the miles of long dirt roads that snake their way up the ridge hardly make it any less cut off. Three creeks flow down from the top, and along each is a road, one of which is not generally passable, and each represents a strung-out but self-contained (by virtue of family ties) community. From the top, where the ground spreads out enough to allow a tiny hillside garden, it is about seven miles to the nearest school (by a dirt road that cannot be crossed in snowy or wet weather), and an almost equal distance to a store where more than a few canned goods can be bought. People must stock up provisions for the winter months; the children cannot reach school. Only a few families have wells, for they must be sunk quite deep to reach the first water sources. The traditional occupation of men on Mud Lick has been cutting timber, when it can be found, and paper wood, poor growth or young trees used to make pulp, when the market price is up, from around their homes. There is little left now that can be cut and sold. Thousands of the surrounding acres have been put under the protection of the National Forest Service. More and more land is constantly being purchased —often from elderly people who surrender the land title at the time of their death—in what is apparently an attempt at the conservation of mountain beauty through buying out whole communities of mountain people. Little thought, it seems, is given to the conservation of the mountains as a place where people can live. Some on Mud Lick mine; some dig coal out of little "dog hole" mines to sell to their neighbors; some still cut paper wood; there are many who draw welfare.

Well, the worst thing about bein' poor, there's a lot o' things. You know poor people, buddy, they live on such a little stuff. They don't have enough money to buy nothin' with very good. They live very hard. Man, I know people that lives very bad, son. You take no money or no jobs to make money off, an' you're gonna be in very bad shape. You don't have nothin' to eat half the time like you oughta have, an' that's a very bad life. You take four or eight kids an' have to live on maybe jest so many food stamps, an' you know you're gonna eat them up pretty directly, an' there you sit. Live very hard.

If a man makes under $3,000 a year an' he's got much of a family, he's very poor, he's a poor man. You know some people don't have $2,000 a year to live on, an' a lot of 'em, you'd say, don't have $1,500. An' they have a little garden maybe. 'Cordin' to your family 'bout how you live. I know three thousand ain't no money now. Used to be, if you had $3,000, you'd be in good shape, but now it's gettin' hard. You go in these supermarkets an' take $15, an' you can pack it out under your arm.

Goose Creek is one of the major little communities in the county. Defined by the last half of a twelve-mile-long black-top road running beside the creek which ties together a network of lesser roads winding back through the mountains and into other counties, Goose Creek claims about sixty homes. Few families are without a large garden because the land there is level and good. Most of the older men on the creek have experienced long years of mining, but few are still willing or able to go back to that work. Almost all of the young men past school age work in other states or have gone to Vietnam. A good number of men here, as in all the county's communities, work for the Concentrated Employment Program's Operation Mainstream at public works jobs. Most of the people on the creek spring from seven or eight main families.

There is a community center near the head of the creek, housing a Head Start classroom for about twenty children and a workshop. It is used for fairly regular community meetings.

Almost everyone on the creek has two trades, of which one is farming. The other might be mining, carpentry, auto mechanics, logging, coal hauling, truck driving, or, a full-time job itself, drawing welfare. Tobacco is the cash crop; hogs are virtually the only stock raised to sell. The community is touched with a less rigid sort of poverty; a life where people raise much of what they eat but where cash incomes are extremely low. There is access, by a passable road, to both schools and town. Yet lack of real money shows itself in homes too frail to withstand the winter cold, too small to shelter properly the large numbers who live in them. The difficulties that the mountains themselves place in the way of economic development are felt here as much as elsewhere: treacherous roads that tear apart cars and trucks and which translate thirty miles into an hour's drive; lack of plumbing and waste disposal which, along with such unnatural things as strip mines, results in spoiled creeks and rivers; floods which destroy the little that men have built; general isolation, by distance, from towns which themselves are isolated from cities; a history of one-room schools—of which there were, until the last few years, three in the Goose Creek area—made necessary by the far-flung communities and at which little was taught.

HOUSING

A more specific sketch of conditions that prevail all over the county can be made by looking at Goose Creek. In the county, 64 per cent of all the housing units are unsound. In Goose Creek, nine out of ten of the homes are not as good as the log houses that some old couples still live in. They are constructed from old lumber, often with just one outside wall and no insulation at all except wallpaper or newspapers and, in rare cases, plasterboard. They are extremely difficult to keep warm in the bitter mountain winters, and, in many structures, no attempt at all is made to heat back rooms like kitchens. Most houses have two rooms and a kitchen, and most families range in size from seven to ten. It is common practice for newly wed couples to live in one- or two-room frames built beside a parent's home. In other communities, conditions are more severe:

Well, I could 'scribe what I seen on the inside. I went there long back. It was sometime last spring. An' I don't believe I ever seed no nastier house in my life, but these are old people. An' I went in, an' I went in the back door an' came through the kitchen. Come through the door to come to a fireplace. An' I'd say it was full of women. Two of 'em was very old, an' one of 'em was in bed. One of 'em had three or four pigs on a bottle. It was very cold. An' I don't know buddy, I coulda took a broom or a shovel an' swept dirt up in the kitchen. They had a wood stove, an' there was ashes all over the place. I believe it's against the health department to have a house such as that. I've never seen such a dirty house. She said her roof leaked, but it was covered with this roofin' paper an' it had lumber under that. Well the walls looked pretty good, but it was a bad house, and the floors, I've never seen such a dirty floor in my life.

Before they fixed it, Jimmy's house, it was a very bad house. It was built low, I had to stoop right over to get in. It was about the worst little house, I mean jest as far as livin' in, it was a bad house. But now he's done some work on it, an' he's fixed it up real nice. Best as I remember it had four rooms an' there must have been about ten children.

Well, I don't want to tell you the names, but I could take you to some houses that's jest box houses. And the floors are bad. You know when I say a box house I mean a house that's jest boxed up out of old lumber, you say, an' got paper on the inside. You got a wall of lumber here, an' nothin' but paper on these walls, then you got a bad house to live in this winter. Sometimes they'll take a little roofin' paper an' put it on the inside, an' that makes it a little bit warmer. But any time you got a box house, jest one box, an' little strips over them cracks, then you've got the worst house you've ever seed. You can't hardly keep them warm; the air'll get in around that. An' there's plenty o' them houses in this country. There's not as many in this creek as there is in the head of Mud Lick or Flat Creek. In Granny's Branch there's several of 'em, I looked at three or four the other day, up a holler where you've never been. I went up there to look at a house way in the head of a holler up there. It'us a bad house.

If you had a real good log house, an' had it notched and daubed . . . . See old people'd build log houses an' daub 'em with clay mud, an' that makes a good warm house. It makes a thick house; you ain't jest got a little inch plank. There's not many of 'em left in this country. I remember my grandaddy way back had a log house, but his was with big thick logs. They was a foot thick or two, an' they hewed 'em out with a broad ax, an' he had that daubed with mud. You

*know when you hew lots of logs down here, you think
you're gettin' them close together, but you're not. You
put a plank inside over that, an' then you fill that outside
in with mud, clay mud, I call it, and smooth it over, an'
you've got a good warm house.*

HEATING

People use coal to heat their homes, and in the winter it
takes about a ton a month to warm even a small house.
That much coal costs eight dollars, and the man who hauls
it charges an extra three dollars on each ton. Coal stoves
burn out at night leaving the walls, which often seem to
do no good at all, as the only protection against the cold outside. Ideally, the tin pipes which take out the smoke should
be replaced each year because the heat from the stove burns
holes in them. When they are not, they become very dangerous, and almost every year someone's house on the creek
will catch fire and burn down. It is not always possible for a
poor man to pay out, all at once, the sixty or seventy dollars
needed to buy enough coal to last the winter. He must take
the chance that when his small supply of coal runs out, the
roads will be clear enough that another one month's load
can reach him.

*Well, if you got plenty of clothes you can keep warm I
guess. They get used to it, but it's mighty hard. But you
know, people gets used to winter as it comes on, an' you
got to have maybe ten, twelve tons of coal. It's mighty hard
fer them people to find it, and a lot o' people have to take
wood in this country. They get by, but it's bad.*

WATER

For water to drink, to cook and to wash with, many people
rely on the small streams that come off the mountains.
They must, of course, walk to get their water, and in the

wintertime they may have to break the ice to fill their bucket. In summer months these streams, and most of the wells, dry up for a time, leaving people waiting days for a rainfall.

If you don't have a well, a lot o' times there'll be a spring. They get it out of a spring or a branch. You could call it a branch. I don't call it a creek. This out here is a creek; it's bigger down here. An' that's where them people gets their water here around. An' you study 'bout how you have to drink water at this time of the year, comin' out of the branch, how warm it is. An' that woman told me how she raised eight or nine kids, an' she's lived up there I guess all her life. An' she has to pack water to wash; she has to pack water to cook with, an' she has to go right up that hill an' pack it straight up and down.

No it's not good. It's not good to drink. It's too much sulferous in it to be good water. But that's all they got.

I wouldn't drink that out of this creek at all, fer it's not good. I wouldn't drink that no way fer it's got things in it above here I wouldn't want to drink. You'd have to go up the hill, or somewhere down the holler. Now you see down this road here is four or five houses, an' they got a well, an' they started haulin' water from here yesterday. Out here they got some outside toilets over it. And they got a strip mine up there that's pushed a lot o' mud down it, an' it stays too muddy an' nasty. We couldn't drink outa that. We used to wash outa that creek down there, before the strip mines ever got started up here. Out by that barn, is a big hole o' water. It stayed there pretty an' clear all summer. But ever since they started that, it stays black an' muddy.

GARBAGE

The standard solution to getting rid of garbage is to drop it in the creek. There is no place else to put it. Most mountain streams that run through inhabited areas are full of cans and bottles, stray auto parts and other refuse. Only animal carcasses are not pushed over the side, for they poison the water. A constant cause for dispute is whether a neighbor's toilet drains into the creek, which is contrary to law.

One of the outstanding sights along mountain roadways is the number of junked and stripped automobile bodies. Driving is so rough on vehicles that to keep one car running requires the parts from several others. Often these empty hulks are turned over into creek beds to shore up the embankments and to divert the rushing water of springtime floods.

Where do they dump it? They dump it anywheres to get it out of the basket. They burn the papers up, and they dump bottles over the creek or anywheres to get shet of it up here. It's not good fer the creeks, but it's the only place I seed. Or on the roads.... You can see old cans dumped over.

No garbage pickup around here; that's what we need. There's no dump or nothin'.

In Goose Creek, there's sixty–seventy homes, and none of 'em's hardly got a inside bathroom.

ROADS

In the mountains, roads—and Clay County's are not exceptions—are terribly bad. Blacktop roads generally stick to the wide bottoms where there is at least a possibility of easy construction and repair. When a major road is forced to wind through and over the mountains, the problems of building it so that sections do not wash away in rainy seasons or rock falls do not cover it are much increased. In the mining areas, the big trucks, loaded far over their legal limits with coal, tear up any roads that they travel. Most people, however, do not live on the blacktops; they live miles and miles up roads that often are a combination of rocky, rutted dirt trails and creek beds. It is no little accomplishment to build a road at all through mountain country, and probably the greater part of the people in Clay County do not find their road passable three months out of the year. It is the poor condition of the roadways that people most often complain about, and it is for roads that taxpayers most willingly see their money spent. Where once, it is said, people valued the inaccessibility of their homes to others, they now argue mightily for a way to get a truck to their door. Such is the change that occurs when people lose, or grow out of, as some would say, their self-sufficiency and begin to require speed of transport and the services of others.

It's hard gettin' out of here in the winter. If it comes a big snow and falls on this road here, we might have to stay up here till it thaws off. Without you put chains on. A lot o' times they grade it, but they don't grade up here like they do on the highway. It's awful bad up these dirt roads. You take this branch right here. If they get ice in that creek, they can't get up in here. Or they might have to walk fer a week or two up that branch. I'm afraid of slick roads.

Course they go to school now better than they used to. Used to, I'd say they didn't go to school three, four, five months a year. But we have better roads now than we used to have. Course when it's too bad up here fer the school buses to run, see, they don't go to school at all. An' they can't drive the bus till it fairs up. An' they make up time in the summer which causes school to run late. But I'd say they go to school now better than they used to. They ride the bus, and they don't drive the bus when it's too dangerous on the kids.

Before you got here, up Granny's Branch was a creek road. Now do you believe that? That means you had to go up the creek all the way to the head of Granny's Branch. The first time I went up Granny's Branch, I went up the

*creek, an' I didn't think I was aimin' to get out o' the creek.
I had that same truck I'm drivin' now, an' it was trees
stickin' over the holler an' I like to hit my mirror on one.
The first time I went up Granny's Branch, I'll tell you why
I went up there. You notice when you go up, the road up
there forks, an' a man lives right in the fork. I heared he
had some hogs to sell, it was in the wintertime, which he
did have the hogs. Well I went up that branch, buddy, an'
I didn't think that I'd ever get up through there. I went
right up to his house an' asked did he have some hogs. I
couldn't buy 'em; he was too high fer me. I asked the man,
"What kind of road you got up here?" and he said, "We
ain't got no road, buddy. We been promised a road fer years
and years." I said, "Buddy that's the one place I've seen
where you ain't got anything." But they built a road in
Granny's Branch when you came here. An' last winter they
filled it out o' that creek, an' it got so muddy an' froze last
winter. I could see it doin' that. But if they put a lot of
gravel on it, they might have a better road. Jesus Christ, that
was the worst road I'us ever on. An' they had to walk out,
all the kids did, to go to school. I guess that's a mile and a
half from the head o' that holler. Maybe two miles. I imagine it's close to forty families. It's more'n that. I guess
forty-five.*

CLOTHES

Mountain winters are cold, and it is a problem that all
must face to provide clothing and shoes for their children.
Often, of course, children are kept from school because
they lack warm coats. Shoes do not last long if the trail
that leads to the store or to the school bus is a muddy or
hard-frozen and rocky branch. Kids run barefoot in the
summertime to save their footwear, and in some households,
even the winter does not mean that children can wear their
shoes after school.

*No, they don't have near enough clothes. Plenty of 'em
don't. I could say one thing, that's the reason a lot of young-
'uns drops out of school. They're very poor, an' they don't
have the right kind of clothes they think they should have to
wear to school. An' 'fore they go to high school they quit.
They can't afford the clothes that maybe someone can
afford, an' they feel very bad about goin' down to where two
or three hundred, or maybe five hundred kids are, an' them
not dressed as well as other people. I've heard people say
that they couldn't send their kids to school because they
didn't have enough clothes to wear.*

*It's plenty o' times in the wintertime that kids'll wear
their shoes out. I have to buy mine maybe two or three pairs
a year. If they get too bad, they're not gonna go to school.
When they get gone they'll say I have to have a pair of
shoes, an' I'll have to manage to get them 'em or they'll quit.*

FOOD

Setting out a good dinner ranks high in mountain traditions. In the summer and fall, when the gardens have borne
well and for some there have been hogs to slaughter, most
eat better and more heartily than do city dwellers. Winter
brings a sparser table, especially for families who had no
garden from which to store up jars of food. Even a family
in good luck can count only on store-bought beans, fresh
milk, and cornbread. A family in "hard times" might sustain itself on biscuits and watery gravy. Meat, with the exception of bologna, is a rarely seen commodity for most. A
large percentage of the people in the county receive food
stamps each month. The help that these give is most times
not great, but they make the difference between cornbread
and cornbread with soup beans.

*You know, I've seed a lot of people who eats very bad.
A lot of people don't have the money to buy what they
need. They might eat good a while, but you take people on*

food stamps. If they don't have a garden—as many people don't have a garden as do—they live pretty hard. They don't have half enough to eat. They can't afford it.

When I say half enough, they may have nothin' but gravy an' biscuits, an' the gravy'll be made up outa water, stirred up out of flour dough an' water. They may not have milk to put in it. You want to have good gravy, you got to have milk an' other stuff to put in it. I went to a place here long back, an' they was eatin' breakfast, an' had nary a thing but gravy an' a little biscuits. And that looked bad to me. They had a great bunch o' kids, but they was eatin' it, very happy seemed to me.

I doubt if they eat meat more'n once a month. If they got it. They'd have to go down to the supermarket to get it, an' it's high. It's the highest thing they got. An' all they got to be careful what they buy to make them food stamps go far enough. You can't buy much meat. If you do, you're gonna run out of money directly.

AGRICULTURE

For many, in the right seasons, there is abundance in the mountains. A good deal is actually raised on the roughly 12 per cent of Clay County that is level. In fact, much is grown on the hillsides that a midwesterner would not consider planting. Families with a little space plant cabbages, beans, tomatoes, corn, potatoes, and cucumbers. That part of the harvest which is not eaten at once is canned for the winter. Blackberries grow wild in the hills and are picked for canning and to sell. Poke, a strange wild plant tasting like turnip or mustard greens, can be picked in the woods. Men raise bees in homemade bee "gums" and try to sell honey. Each spring and fall, those who have hogs slaughter them for meat, and pigs are sold to neighbors for ten dollars apiece. Calves, however, are not killed for beef, but rather sold in London, Kentucky, at the stock market. There is a feeling that God put hogs on the earth to be eaten, but that cows were put here to give milk and not to be killed by those who raise them.

Years ago, before there were stock laws and before blight destroyed the chestnut trees, hogs were allowed to roam free on the hills and fatten themselves on nuts for the fall slaughter. Now, when owners must take upon themselves the responsibility of raising their own stock, most cannot afford the expense and must forego the pleasure of fresh meat. The only real cash crop that is grown is burley tobacco, but the government makes strict allotments of the amount a farmer can grow. Not every farmer who wants one can get an allotment, or "tobacco base." Most of the tobacco bases held by poor men are in the neighborhood of 7/100 of an acre to 3/10 of an acre. The crop grown on 7/100 of an acre might bring eighty to one hundred dollars. Tobacco prices are very high, but it is also very costly to raise as it must be repeatedly sprayed and fertilized, and stored in barns to dry out for weeks after cutting, and in the winter-time the land must be sown with a good cover crop like rye grass. Another source of income, for those with the time to go after it, is the collecting of medicinal roots— ginseng, apple root, May root, corn root, and others which can be sold to medicine manufacturers. Ginseng, the most valuable, brings about three dollars an ounce.

Basically, this is the extent of agriculture in Clay County. The mountains are unsuited to the plow, yet the plow has broken that rocky land for well over one hundred years.

HEALTH

All diseases and health problems that plague men in our relatively sanitary society are seen in amazing proportions in Clay County. The mines and the rigors of mountain life have made their contribution—pulmonary diseases, back and bone infirmities, and all manner of crippling injuries—

to the general unhealthiness seen in mountain communities. Problems such as tuberculosis, intestinal worms, sugar diabetes, and malnutrition often enter serious stages before they are diagnosed because people are frequently hard put to travel to doctors and to pay their bills. Most medical treatment is extremely impersonal; it is administered through state agencies for public health and mental health, tuberculosis clinics, or by overworked physicians with claim to far too few hospital beds. In Clay County there are two private hospitals—one of which is church supported—and together these are staffed by five doctors. In addition there are three doctors in Manchester. Though this is barely adequate for the twenty thousand people in Clay County, there is the additional load from Jackson County, where there is only one doctor and no hospital. In 1969 Clay County broke ground for a new hospital, but even when it is completed, most patients will still have to report to those places where treatment is inexpensive: the small Red Bird Mission Hospital in Clay County, and the Appalachian Regional hospitals in Harlan and Pineville—all over an hour's drive from most points in the county.

Though mothers are diligent in their attempts to keep their children neat, the notion of cleanliness has little bearing in the mountains where in cold winter even the air is heavy with coal smoke. Unsanitary conditions, certainly increased by outside toilets, polluted streams, and lack of garbage disposal, strengthen the foothold of disease in mountain communities. Homes that cannot be heated in winter, insufficient clothing, poor food—all play a role.

Though most women have their babies delivered by doctors in one of the hospitals, Clay County has an infant death rate of 45.7, which lists fourth from the top among the 120 counties in Kentucky.

County doctors handle emergency cases as best they can, often sending accident victims by ambulance to the hospital at the University of Kentucky in Lexington, one

hundred miles away. Patients suffering from the usual
range of problems see doctors on a first-come, first-served
basis in the hospitals. On busy days, it requires several hours
of waiting to see a physician.

*A lot of people seems to be more sick than they was when
I was growin' up. Seems to me like they weren't a'goin'
every day to the doctors like they are now. Half the people
you see it seems are sick or say they are, an' they're goin'
to see the doctor.*

*I couldn't offhanded tell you how many's got it, but a lot
of people's got the sugar diabetes. Lot of people's got TB.
But I'd say more people's got the sugar diabetes than they
have that. Tell me if you don't let the TB get too big a
start on you, you can cure the TB pretty quick. But I don't
know, I never had it I reckon, an' never had the sugar
diabetes, or if I had, I didn't know it. I'll tell you about
that. That sugar diabetes is a bad disease. You know it does
people awful bad. A lot o' times you have to have one of
your legs cut off, or one of your feet took off. It's a bad
disease.*

*Yeah we got worms. We used to have worm medicine,
they had it in bottles way back, but now you go to the
drugstore, you can buy different kinds. My mother used to
get it in the bottles. Christ, it'us the worst tastin' stuff I
ever seed in my life. I'd rather do anythin' than take a dose
o' that. Now they got different stuff; it don't taste so bad.
If it gets bad enough you can go see a doctor. There's
different kinds of worms: pin worms and big worms. They'll
kill you too, brother, if you don't get them out. I've seed
kids had 'em pretty bad. They had to go to the doctor to
get 'em out. Lots of kids have worms in this country.*

WELFARE SYSTEM

All welfare recipients and unemployed fathers are allowed
medical cards for their families. These provide for general

medical treatment and some hospital care, the money coming through the welfare department under the category of Aid to Families with Dependent Children. Unfortunately, Kentucky claims to be unable to meet the demands of the program and is curtailing it throughout the state.

In general, the welfare system in Kentucky is no worse, no more arbitrary, or more bureaucratic than anywhere else. It is a victim of the same extraordinarily confining categories of assistance that all states must work within, and the same ill-timed rulings that the federal government sets forth—such as the recent freeze on the size of the Aid to Families with Dependent Children grants that state may receive. In Mississippi, the means by which the AFDC regulations can be used against recipients—such as the notorious midnight raids on homes to see that no man lives there—have been much heralded. In Kentucky, where the number of injured and disabled men in their twenties, thirties, and forties is staggering, much the same is the case with the categories of the Aid to the Permanently and Totally Disabled and AFDC-Incapacity. In the former category, a claimant must prove that he is permanently and totally unable to perform any substantial gainful activity. Neither partial nor temporary disability can be compensated for by reason of the federally defined category. Thus an applicant, who may be bedridden, is forced to see doctors who, for the welfare department's fee of five dollars, are expected to make comprehensive judgments about their patient's ability to work. If a doctor does affirm that the patient is permanently and totally disabled, then the welfare department will send him to a State Examining Physician, usually in Lexington, who frequently will conclude from the same medical evidence that the applicant is only totally and temporarily disabled or permanently and partially disabled, thus collapsing the applicant's case. To contest this, the applicant must produce more medical reports indicating disability than the department can produce indicating fitness.

If a man has enough Social Security quarters to apply for benefits under that agency's APTD category, he must prove that he is unable to engage in substantial gainful activity anywhere within the *national economy*. Applicants are sometimes told that they could be trained for a type of work done in Texas or Oregon. These glaring absurdities, it seems, have not yet impressed themselves on the lawmakers of this country.

Perhaps the most humane program to aid those unable to work is welfare's AFDC-Incapacity. To receive benefits under this category, a father or mother must only prove inability to return to a former occupation, which for men is most often mining, or to perform any other gainful activity in the county or community. Difficulties here are that single or childless men are not eligible for benefits and that "other gainful activity" is often construed to mean night watchman or service station attendant, which are jobs that few but the bedridden could not theoretically perform.

None of these programs takes the availability of employment into consideration. That a given job exists, whether or not it is available, is a sufficient criterion for denying a man welfare. That seems to be a theory running throughout all programs of assistance to the disabled—that a man is morally responsible to perform a job until his dying breath, and that state agencies are morally responsible to keep a man from spending a single more relaxed day than can be helped. Is it unfair to assume that the working men who have done the heavy labor of this country deserve a little more leisure—if that is what you can call the state a man with a disarranged spine or rock dust finds himself in—than Sunday off once a week? How greatly does it increase the productivity of our labor force to run an injured man through a mill of doctor's exams, welfare fieldworker's inquiries and home visits, and a lengthy, humiliating appeals process for the sake of determining that he can still stand and therefore might still be able to chalk up six more months on the job?

In some ways, the Kentucky welfare system excels in comparison with those of other states. Payments to families with dependent children are based on 87 per cent of a fifteen-year-old standard of living scale, whereas in Mississippi, the ceiling is 27 per cent. Yet while many cities and states have taken upon themselves the expense of non-federally sponsored programs like general public assistance, Kentucky has no such category.

The state, like all others, offers unemployment compensation to those who swear they are able and available to work. To receive benefits (Rocking Chair pay) or to get a medical card on the grounds of unemployment, a man cannot refuse any job offered him. This provides a complication for a disabled man, denied welfare, who has registered with the employment office only to get medical assistance, for, while he is in fact disabled, he must assert that he can and will take any job offered him. The employment offices administer a Manpower Training and Development program which requires for admission a level of education which few have reached. The Bureau of Rehabilitation Services, which does the bulk of the vocational training and re-training in the state, forces men to leave their homes to attend the training sites, which for some might be several counties away. All training programs are faced with the fact that there are virtually no private, non-mining jobs in the mountains, and what jobs there are are heavily competed for by the young.

I Rocked about three times to my knowin's. Never drawed no welfare. Never got no food stamps. And way back, I got a little commodity, you know. You know when

*they first bring it in here, I got some of it one or two times,
I was drawin' some Rockin' Chair money. An' they wouldn't
let me have commodity. Said I was drawin' too much.
"Well OK," I said, "Keep it."*

How It Feels to Be Poor

The poor people of Kentucky have been made subject
to an incredible number of programs designed for their
betterment. All of Franklin D. Roosevelt's great plans were
tested in the mountains. All manner of public works
projects have been here and gone. Where the WPA left
off the Happy Pappies (some twenty-five years later) began,
and when that program ended the Nelson and Mainstream
programs rushed in. Public assistance has probably achieved,
in spite of itself, record caseloads here. And surely the
rediscovery of Appalachia had great effect on the creation
of President Johnson's War on Poverty. Kentucky has seen
a missionary movement, a union movement, and repre-
sentatives of the Southern Conference Educational Fund,
the Christian Appalachian Movement, the Council of
Southern Mountains, the Save the Children Federation,
the Appalachian Volunteers, the Volunteers in Service
to America, and literally scores of other organizations trying to promote their solutions to the mountains' problems
and, in rare cases, trying to effect the solutions that the
poor themselves have devised. Appalachia, and Kentucky
more than other states, and Clay County as much as any
county, have been worked over to a greater extent than
even prime areas like Mississippi and Harlem or even the
lands of the American Indians. The main thrust of these
agencies and groups has been to improve the hillbilly
through give-away programs—that people are often forced
by circumstance to participate in or are degraded by having
to fight to participate in—or by channeling the people's
energy through the often fallacious theories and plans of

an outsider who considers he knows "the way" or "a way" toward a better life. There have been some notable exceptions to this, many of which have been provided by the inspirations of indigenous people working for several of the already mentioned organizations.

There have also been, unfortunately, a lot of examples of an outsider damaging the spirit that moves people of a community to strike out for a better life. One Clay County man, not an organizer but simply a coal truck driver with some insights into the problems he and his neighbors face, complained that his community had been virtually wrecked through the efforts of a VISTA worker. The organizer, he said, succeeded in exciting the people about the things they could do if they met together and acted together. At the first gathering people began talking with each other about the ways of cleaning up the community's creeks and roads. At the next meeting, however, the organizer had something else on her mind and lectured the people on that. Community interest and the organization itself deteriorated as, at each subsequent meeting, the organizer dominated the discussion, which was always about some new topic of her choosing. People lost interest in coming to meetings and have since resisted all other attempts by outsiders to "organize them."

It is the observation of one long-time community worker in the mountains that the outside organizers have maintained a fine record of discouraging militancy among poor people. He believes that it is the natural reaction of an organizer when presented, for example, with a situation where disgruntled welfare claimants decide to march around the courthouse carrying shotguns to emphasize their grievances, to argue that that is a bad plan, which could only lead to arrest, and to point out that it is not so correct an approach as petitioning, getting legal help, etc. What occurs in a case like that is that poor people bow to the voices of "wisdom," as they have been trained to follow the dictates of whoever is educated and sophisticated and are deterred from testing out which of the approaches to a problem are in fact wise, and which will be effective. They have been denied a chance to learn how they can accomplish their goals by an outsider who has theories of his own about how things should be done. It would be better if people exercised the methods that come naturally to them—better that they march around the courthouse, get arrested, and then decide, on that basis, whether that is the best tactic—than that they do nothing but follow the advice of one educated outsider about how they can free themselves from the rule of the more polished individuals, welfare workers, politicians, and program planners who make the decisions which control the lives of the poor.

The kinds of political activity that mountain poor people have engaged in when they have followed their own inclinations have been more militant and no less successful than movements arranged by outsiders. In 1969, a group of Whitely County citizens, angered that their pleas for repair on a road used by all and by school buses were consistently ignored, elected to declare the road unsafe for travel and to close it off. They set up road blocks and refused to let traffic pass. As each group of men were arrested, others appeared to take their place. Finally a much embattled highway department agreed to resurface the road.

The struggle against strip mining was largely carried out at the direction of mountain people. The real commitment on the part of the men everywhere in the mountains to put a stop to the terrible waste caused by surface mining was a stronger showing of the real wants of the mountain people than anything that has been seen since. Though they were not successful in their main purpose of outlawing stripping on mountain slopes, they did force strip mines into the most costly battle they have ever had to wage.

It is essential that people can learn from their own efforts how change can be won. Most programs and program planners have failed to see that oppression is not primarily a matter of little money and bad homes: it is essentially a problem of a people's spirit. Giving people money and rebuilding homes is a good and generally necessary thing, but no one has yet come up with the wherewithal to give all poor mountain people good incomes and nice homes. Although most programs aspire to provide pathways that will lead people out of poverty, the planners seem to forget that they are manhandling people's lives. They try to give new tools to people, yet they are foreign tools and make people ashamed of the tools they themselves have. They try to impose, by fragments, the features of a modern America on communities with very beautiful, if old-fashioned, cultures. At every step, each little bit of modernity is met with resistance by a much larger force of old methods of doing and thinking of things. Those bent on obliterating poverty can either overpower it—and the culture and traditions that go with it—by constructing a thousand factories and a million homes in the mountains, or they can seek other ways, not the least of which might be ending the humiliating, self-righteous programs our government now operates. It might be better to let the poor go it alone and try to solve their problems in their own way than to dispatch them bits and pieces of the good life —a little adult education here, a little welfare there. Hopefully, while the government concerns itself with some of the most severe material elements of poverty—bad food, bad clothing, bad homes—the poor people of the mountains will continue to use their wits to overcome a world seemingly bent on showing its superiority to them.

OEO: Almost all programs and outsiders seem, intentionally or not, to try to impress upon the mountaineer the error of his ways, or the boat that he is missing. As an example, OEO is here singled out, in part because it is the least offender.

The Office of Economic Opportunity came to Kentucky in the form of multi-county Community Action programs, or CAP's, whose boards of directors were filled with professional and political townspeople. In the Cumberland River Valley, of which Clay County is a part, there was begun, in 1964, an eight-county "politicians'" CAP. Poor people's groups throughout the area fought against this, and by dint of their own persistence, succeeded in persuading OEO to defund the monolith in 1966. In its place were set up four single- and double-county groups, one being the Jackson-Clay Community Action Agency, whose boards were made up almost entirely of low-income people. Thus the organized poor had succeeded in bringing home to themselves what was to be the master solution to poverty. In Clay County, the CAP helped to set up local community poor people's groups to which VISTA volunteers were dispatched. The efforts of almost all organizers and organizations were aimed at implementing the CAP structure of board-controlled community groups, organization presidents, parliamentary procedure, etc.

But the idea had two main failings. One was that, while attempting to be a grass-roots organization, it was forced by the nature of OEO's own programs to be a top-down arrangement. Community organizers were mostly outsiders, or dominated by outsiders, and it was their job locally to implement OEO projects. But these were projects not designed by mountain people, and it is likely they were designed not with the mountains, but with the nation, in mind; and they were hopelessly complex. Who in a poor community can handle the intricate job of writing proposals, reading guidelines, locating personnel, and preparing budgets? Even though they sit on the boards that approve the programs, how can they gain a feeling of control of or participation in operating these programs? For most

of the poor people, the CAP has become another agency—
though by far the most benign one—that has taken a hand
in running their lives.

The other failing is the sadder one. Almost all of the
efforts of the organized poor are channeled into or directed
by the CAP. When it comes down to it, the CAP's are not
prepared to fight the many fronts of poverty. All that they
are able to do is to administer OEO programs such as
child care, but only for a few, Emergency Food vouchers,
but not for all, Self-Help programs like home improvement,
but not for all, certain home services like sewing classes,
the VISTA program, and a few others. It cannot engage
itself in many activities, notably political ones, and has
little contact with the sort of problems that poor men
come up with when they talk informally out in the fields.
If the welfare department were controlled by poor people,
it would still only be equipped to administer welfare. OEO
is another grand project aimed at eradicating, in some
measure, the visible aspects of poverty. Its often ill-tailored
programs are planned in Washington and obviously not by
poor people. It is not geared to learning the desires of the
poor, and it would probably be prohibited by law from
meeting those desires if it knew them.

Town and Country: One problem faced by those who
run agencies to benefit the poor is the ingrained prejudice
of the mountain poor against towns, town dwellers, all
the things that are done in town and at the courthouse,
and men, except preachers, who wear ties. It is a general
feeling that the people in town, who are usually the middle
class, care little about the poor, do not want to hear them,
and believe themselves better than those in the country.
Many come to take on the assumption that townspeople
are right—this is the most degrading and probably most
destructive part of poverty. Those people who have made
it, who have money in the bank, do not much care for you,

think you were born to serve, treat you as subhuman, and in time succeed in convincing you that that is what you are. But not quite, because most poor people retain a spark within them that makes them burn with bitterness and resentment toward those with economic and political power. The gratification that fills a man after he has joined a successful mine strike or the boycott of a white-owned store in the South, pays for years of indignities, of feeling shabby, uneducated, inarticulate, clumsy, of being poor. It is this sort of striking out that eases the real burdens of poverty.

Sure I can see a lot o' diff'rence in the poor man an' the well-off man in how they treat him. I think a lot o' times, the big feller, they want to keep the poor man down anyway. They want to keep him down so maybe he can depend on them. An' they want him to stay poor probably so they can tell him what to do. So he'll listen to them, and they'll get his vote. Sometimes I think the poor people's been treated pretty bad. Take the big shots, they'll shake hands with you every four years, and you're a good man. But after that four years, you probably don't see them again till the next four years. They've been treated bad. See, they don't get up in the hollers to see how people live. They stay downtown. But every four years they come up in the hollers, an' they see, an' you're fine people then. They're wantin' your votes.

The good things about livin' around here are you're out from a town, an' you don't see much goin' on. You don't hear all that noise you hear about town. It's very quiet an' a diff'rent place than town. That's the reason I say it's a very good place. I don't like to live in a town myself. It's all crowded up. I don't have nothin' against town people myself, but I don't like to live there. It's less botherin' you here. I know it suits me better, an' I know most o' the people'd rather live up here than down in Manchester.

III Political Powerlessness,
the "Courthouse Gang"

It is not strange that poor people in the mountains should feel some distrust and dislike for those who run the towns. They have been badly treated, in a very obvious way, by the political and economic powers that be. The Kentucky political system on the county level, like that of a few other states in the East, remains essentially colonial. Local government is supposed to rest in the hands of the elected county judge and four magistrates, or squires, who are elected by districts. Each magistrate, who is not required to have legal training, is empowered to judge minor suits, mainly traffic cases, that arise in his district and to levy fines. The county judge, who also may not have legal training, presides over most cases that arise in the county. Together the magistrates and the judge administer all county revenue and much of the federal and state money that comes in for such things as roads. These men join other important officials—the high sheriff, the county court clerk, the circuit court clerk, and the county and commonwealth attorneys—in deciding what goes on in their county.

In the past, mine operators played a great part in county politics because the courthouse is in charge of things like assessing coal lands for taxes, road maintenance, attracting or discouraging outside industry, and enforcing the tonnage limits on coal trucks. However, as the number of men engaged in mining, and thus the number that would be susceptible to company pressure, has declined, so has the direct influence of the individual operators diminished. In their place has come an equally powerful force, the School System. By virtue of its permanently employing far more men and women than any other agency or industry, it has become the seat of power in Clay and most other mountain counties. It is generally thought that the school superintendent, who in Clay County has been in office for years, dictates most of what is done by other county officials as well as how money is spent. In Clay County that power is further compounded by the fact that the husband of the school superintendent is the chairman of the county Republican party, which is by far the stronger party in the county. The school superintendent is not elected but is appointed by the five school board members, who could not themselves be elected without the support of the incumbent school superintendent. Political power, which is centered in the figures of the school superintendent, county judge, magistrates, and county court clerk, is built upon all the votes of the county and town employees, state highway department employees, welfare recipients, and school system employees, and is maintained throughout the county by a network of minor politicos who are entrusted with rallying support during election campaigns. The resulting situation for the poor is one in which nothing seems to come down to them from their local governments and there is no immediate way apparent to get anything out of their local governments, which, it is clear, are main elements of political oppression.

Election time, which in Clay County means the Republican primary, is heralded months in advance by the appearance everywhere of candidates' posters and stickers. The public campaign is quite exciting, and it is cause for much heated discussion out in the country—reviving old feuds, suspicions, and grievances concerning the candidates. For some offices, like jailer or coroner, there are often as many as a dozen men and women running, each backed by his or her own nucleus of family and friends. Elections, like most other important matters in the county, are very much involved with family allegiances. The mountain voter puts great weight on pleas for support by "my wife's daddy's cousin," and considerable respect is accorded to the bearer of certain distinguished names. Often a candidate enjoys a victorious campaign by letting his wife's family do the work for him, and, on occasion, a father with a good deal of pull will do the campaigning for his relatively unknown son. Before the election there are mass rallies at the county's larger schools where all candidates may speak. These are usually the scene of loud and underhanded debates between the various contenders for an office. Every so often the audiences get enough into the spirit of the occasion that fights or even shootings flare up. During the campaign, the candidates cover as much ground as possible, slapping as many backs and shaking as many hands as are presented to them across the county.

A private campaign is also waged by the hangers-on to the political bosses. There are men in each community who at every election time come out on the side of the incumbent and go around to their neighbors handing out campaign cards and, where it will do any good, passing out money for assurances of a right vote at the ballot box. It has been said that, in the past, word was spread to welfare recipients and men on county and state payrolls that they were expected to vote the party choices—mostly twenty-year men—back in, but even without being told, most of these men and women feel their own vulnerability and would vote the old ticket for fear of repercussions if they did not. In such a manner is political power won in the mountains. No one quite understands why control over the county's purse strings holds such attraction for men in politics, but it is widely believed that big payoffs go with the jobs to enable officials to leave office more wealthy than they entered and seemingly to spend more money on campaigns than they make in salary.

County officials could not, probably, do all of the things poor people think they should do even if they were not, as it is thought, "crooked." But there remain many areas where, by its inactivity, the "courthouse gang" does its part to keep poor people poor, and many instances where it acts more for the continuance of its own power than in the interests of the approximately 70 per cent of the people in Clay County who are poor. The county does not lobby the state for extensive strip mine control or wider workmen's compensation coverage. The county puts little pressure on an equally uninterested state highway department to pave roads or to build or properly maintain roads through poor communities—unless there is the desire to consolidate power in a certain area. The county judge, who must assign Operation Mainstream men to jobs, puts them to work sweeping schoolhouses and county buildings rather than planning jobs that might actually train men for something. Highway jobs, a traditional source of patronage, do not go to the very poor, but rather to men at peace, more or less, with the business or political powers. The school system, which once locked community people out of the county schoolhouses to keep them from meeting to discuss the ills of the first Cumberland Valley CAP, now, in Goose Creek of Clay County, has refused the community's request for adult education classes in a well-lighted, heated, and spacious community building and offered instead to allow classes to be held in an ancient one-room schoolhouse nearby. The school system, too, casts covetous glances at the CAP-run Head Start program. When the school board administered a Head Start program in the summer of 1969, many thought that the staff hired to run the centers could have been drawn from needier families. Clearly there are things that the government of Clay County could do for the poor yet there is nothing in its recent history of which it could be rightly said, "This was to benefit the poor people."

In the past three or four years it's been the school system, the county judge, the circuit court clerk, the county attorney

*. . . the school system. How come they got the power? Well,
they stayed in office so long. An' the school system is the
biggest . . . it hires more people than any other thing in
Clay County. They got more jobs. An' they got people
teachin' school, an' they got people doin' jobs that the
school superintendent tells, "You vote for this man right
here." Then he's got that kind of power, an' he can go to
the county judge an' say, I put that man in there an' you'll
do what I say.*

*The school superintendent is elected by the school board,
an' they got these districts set up where they know they got
the most people workin'. An' it's very hard to beat 'em
out. But I think the day's comin'.*

*We got five school board members in Clay County.
You take three of them an' you can hire a school superintendent. Other two might be agin her, I don't know. But
she's got the power over 'em. They stand with her. And
they're gonna promise to hire her or they're not gonna get
elected. An' when the board members get elected, they
hire the school system. If they don't do what she says, she'll
put them out in the next two or three years. An' I knowed of
one board member who's been in there since I knowed him.
An' he ain't got out an' run a campaign nowheres. He jest
sat an' rocked on his porch. They elected him. All he got
to say is, "You've got the school board, you'll be the superintendent." That's where they get their power.*

Politics is enjoyed with great intensity in mountain
counties. The personalities and actions of officials, who for
the most part stay quite aloof from their constituents, can
provoke honest hatred among mountain men. In the last
ten years one or two Kentucky mountain counties have lost
their courthouses to arsonists. In 1969, the sheriff of Clay
County was killed by a shotgun blast on a back road after
his successor had already been elected.

The politics of the county are not democratic, except in that word's crudest sense. Entreaties from the poor for better roads and bridges, for more free lunches in school, are generally ignored or put off by claims of too little money, which, in some cases, are true. In fact, the county does not need to serve the organized poor: county officials already satisfy enough people to get elected—by dispensing little loans, gifts, or services, though often only by taking advantage of a man's poverty. And they are not especially eager to encourage greater participation in government. They sometimes, however, overestimate the strength of their positions. In the 1969 primary, a candidate pledging to "serve all the people" and urging voters not to be pushed around by political "bosses," ousted the incumbent county judge, a man who had held that office for twenty years, by twelve votes. There was considerable shock over the outcome of that race, and some speculation that the new county judge would move to redraw the voting precincts used in school and county elections, which were gerrymandered in 1962 to the benefit of the loyal school board members who choose the superintendent.

No, I've never seed nobody jest throw money out an' give nobody; they slip it. They go around behind a car, an' you can see 'em goin' to that car like bees. Now that's somethin' I never did pay much attention to. I knowed they was buyin' it, but I never ask around in a man's business an' try to see him handin' out money to someone. Which I don't like. That money comes off our county. You know if you buy an office, it's yours, an' it'll take you four years to get your money back. That's why a lot o' times you don't get nothin' done in your county for four years. Takes him four years to get his money back.

You know, it has been, they'll say you vote this way or we'll take you off welfare. Well they've caught up with

*that, an' now they're about afraid to tell people somethin'
that's false. They can't take you off 'cordin' to how you
vote, but they used to say they could.*

I think if we had a man to do the job, an' enough
knowledge, an' he come out o' the head o' these hollers
as poor as could be, I think he'd have more feelin' for the
poor people. An' if he had any money to do anythin' with,
like buildin' roads, the county, you know, builds roads, I
think he'd be a'tryin' to build some roads up in these hollers
an' not waste it. Somebody who's up an' got a lot o' money,
they're not carin' 'bout the poor man. If they are, I've not
seed too many of 'em. An' I think that the poor man would
be a'feelin' fer the other poor men.

The reason there's never been a poor man elected is he's
never had a chance. He didn't have no money, an' actually,
I don't agree with buyin' votes myself, there wouldn't be no
use in his a'runnin'. They'd laugh at him. "He can't run
that county judge's office noway. He can't get it, an' he
don't need it noway." He can't get it if he don't have no
money to buy nobody with. That's a pretty bad thing to
say. If you have to buy a vote to win. I won't sell my vote.
I'll vote fer the man that'll do fer the poor people.

I'd like to see a poor man in the county judge's office. If
he had enough ability, enough experience, to do the job.
I don't think poor people'd laugh at him noway. The county
judge we've had has not been too rich a man, but he's been
handled by these people. He'd a been a pretty good man,
but he let other people tell him what to do. You know,
money can hurt or money can help. You know the poor
people don't have money to go down there an' offer the
county judge, an' maybe somebody like the school system
has an' can say you do this or that. I'm against the big shots
takin' over. We need the poor people in office.

It's been some people's wore the seats out in the school
buses. They never gets a new man. They keep that same

bunch on an' on. An' that's the reason they're goin' down the drain. Poor people's wakin' up today, an' they're gonna put them out. I'd say in a couple of years there'll be a new bunch. I don't think that no office is made for one person to stay in a lifetime. There's some new ideals needs to be scattered around.

One thing that makes an oppressive political system harder to fight in the mountains, than say, in the southwest counties of Mississippi where Mrs. Geneva Collins, Charles Evers, and some others have won hard election battles, is that the arm of mountain politics reaches well into poor communities, while in the South, the old political powers never sought any involvement in the black community. In Kentucky it is much harder to isolate the true villains in the political structure, for there is not the separation of black and white, nor really even of rich and poor. There are many fairly poor people in local office and many extremely poor men who cater to their wishes by campaigning for them. The ones who hang around the courthouse and fraternize with the county court clerk are mostly old men with government pensions—and they are actually important parts of the political machine: they control votes. In every poor community are men who would turn over the people's votes to incumbents, which is to say that most poor people in poor communities are related to someone who believes himself to carry some weight in the courthouse. Of course, there are not a whole lot of rich people in Clay County. And many poor men run for jobs like jailer because it is one of the few things that offers a good steady income. All of this means not that the county officials have the needs of the poor at heart, but rather that the poor have a more difficult time arranging themselves to challenge the system itself. Almost everyone in the mountains is poor, and common expectation is that if a less than wealthy man is clever enough to swing a majority vote, he will try, while in office, to get every dollar he can to enrich himself, and this expectation of the people is not usually dashed.

STATEMENT OF PROTEST

I think it's come a time when the poor people's got to wake up. They've got to go a'doin' somethin' about this, place o' lettin' people run everythin' over them. I've seen people run over poor people all my life, an' I'm gettin' tired of it fer my part.

You take in this county right here; they're good people long as you go down an' vote fer 'em. Then they'll come back in the next four years an' pat you on the back an' say, "We're gonna give you jobs." You never see 'em no more— till the next four years. Then you'll see 'em come up. "Well, it's the election. You gonna vote fer old man Charlie this time?" Well, a lot of them will go down there, an' they'll ease around, an' they'll do this, an' they'll say they're Christians. Then they'll reach around there, an' they'll give 'em two dollars, an' people'll stick it in their pockets. An' they'll vote four years against their own interests fer two an' a half or two dollars. That's right. They ought not to do that. They ought to be votin' fer a man who'll do some-thin' fer them. If you can find him. If you got a man in four years doesn't do nothin' fer you, put him out, an' put in a man that will do it. Jest keep on till you try to find that kind o' man. That's the way I see the poor people's gonna have to do. If they don't, they're gonna be trod right down on their feet, an' these big politicians'll jest be cheatin' them alive to get 'em to vote fer 'em every four years . . . . That's right, buddy, I know it. I'm gettin' sick about it.

An' we got the poorest folk there ever was. An' they'll come around an' say, "Let's have a community meetin'." I've been goin' to community meetin's fer the last four years, an' we got plenty people goin' out to meetin's. I ain't got anythin' to offer 'em myself. I'm gonna be honest about that. I ain't got nothin'. But we got people who got money, the OEO. They'll say, "We'll do somethin' about it. You set up a meetin' an' we'll do somethin'." An' when you set that meetin' up, you'll never see 'em about it, an' they'll never do nothin' about it. We talked about buyin' a well rig. People's drinkin' out o' the creek in Clay County, out o' the branches, an' they got Self-Help money to buy a well rig, an' I don't know what's the reason they won't buy it. I believe if I had the money I'd buy it. I wouldn't stop till I found it.

I don't know what to do about it. We oughta jest walk down an' say, "Stop all of it," say, "Boys, this is the time to change over. We come atter you." You believe that'd work? I think that's the only way you're gonna solve the problems.

Now I believe in people havin' jobs. An' that's the only way you can solve the problem a lot o' times. But if you go an' give one man $12,000 or $14,000 a year to run the CAP an' the poor people are gettin' nothin', that's not right either. Why don't you pay a man a salary he can live at, an' take some o' that 12,000 you're givin' him an' let that come down to the poor people to give them somethin'. And the poor people are livin' on $1500, some of 'em a thousand. They're scratchin' any way to get by.

And them Mainstream men, they got jobs sweepin' schoolhouses. They need takin' out o' the schoolhouse though. They need takin' out o' this an' get up there an' build roads an' bridges where people won't have to wade the creek to their knees. Our taxpayers pay fer the schools to be cleaned. They're knockin' people out o' jobs.

And what makes me so sick, the school system won't have nothin' to do with the CAP much. If they got a community building, they want people to go down yonder to the schoolhouse fer adult education class. A woman told me yesterday she wouldn't go. Then she told me she'd go to adult education if it weren't up at the schoolhouse. I told her I wasn't gonna go up to the schoolhouse. We're gonna have it in our own buildin'. We've got a buildin' in Goose Creek. We built it. An' that's where we're gonna hold our meetin's at. What's the reason they can't have it in this center? We got lights. We got plenty o' water in here.

Q. How much do they pay the county judge and the school superintendent?

The county judge? I don't know what they pay him. I don't know what they pay the school superintendent. $7,000, $8,000 a year. I understand they're raisin' it, but I guess the judge'll make around $6,000 a year.

Q. How much do they spend on campaigns?

Oh God! About $20,000, $30,000 every four years. He stays there every year, an' it takes him four years to get that money back. If you buy an office here, you see, you've got to stay there four years to get your money back, about it. They don't get it all off o' the county. They get part of it, but they get other things. That's the reason they don't do nothin'; they got to get that money back. An' that's the way the school system is; they buy it. But they don't be out as much on their politics as the county judge would. They got their districts cut up where they can get elected where they pull. But that day's comin' where they won't have that.

See a good man ain't got a chance. A poor man ain't got a chance now. That's the way they run it, an' that's the way they've had it. It wouldn't be worth nothin' to run down here fer an office. Why they'd jest laugh at me. "Why he ain't got no money." And I've knowed a lot of poor men to run, an' they jest laughed, "Oh, that man can't make it." No wonder he couldn't make it. He didn't have the money to back him. I ain't a'figurin' on runnin' fer nothin'. It wouldn't be no use. I ain't got no money. The people's goin' to have to get behind the election office an' say, "Look here, buddy, that's agin the law." We're gonna have to get shet o' these people, though, that's been a'doin' that an' elect new people. An' then we're gonna stop all that.

I'll tell you the reason the people takes the two dollars. You know, two dollars looks pretty big to the poor man when he's got nothin' to live on. You know, they go to the election, they know they're gonna get the two dollars that day. But they don't have no promise fer a job the day atter. An' I think that if everybody was up on the standard of livin', that they would turn that two dollars down.

You take a poor man today that ain't got a sack o' meal in his house or somethin' like that, two dollars looks pretty big to him. But I wouldn't take the two dollars myself. I'd beg the two dollars 'fore I'd sell my vote fer two dollars. I'd say, buddy, I ain't got a bite, but I don't want your two dollars. But you know a lot o' poor people does that, an' that's a bad thing. I'd like to see that broke up. But one thing that'd do it is fer poor people to get on their feet. They wouldn't be beholdin' to people. Then they'd say we don't have to sell out. We got the money. We've got a job. I believe that'd be one of the answers. I see a poor man, he's got a big bunch o' kids, two or three dollars will help him a big lot sometimes. I've seed the time myself if I had three dollars it'd help me a lot. Sure have.

You know buddy, you take a lot o' these rich people, they want to stay in power. I don't think we should have selfishness, selfish people. I think we should have all alike. But we've got some people that's got respect of persons an' that's all right with your relations, but I don't think that you should go down in that county judge's office an' make diff'rences in people, I think that you should treat everybody alike. You should not send a bulldozer down to the lower end of the county and maybe blacktop a road and never send one to the head of Goose Creek in four years. That's not treatin' your tax money right.

These fellers have been in power so long, an' they got a certain bunch o' people. That's the way they get 'em to stick to 'em. They do that much fer so many people. An' the poor people, they don't do nothin' fer the poor people. The only thing they look at is every four years. You're good people fer three or four months; they shake hands with you to beat the world. An' atter the election, they won't shake hands with you till the next four years. I can tell jest as good, if I fergit about an election, when it's comin' up. They go shakin' hands with you, buddy, an' you know somethin' up. They're out to get elected again. An' if the poor people'd stay away from those elections . . . . They oughta wake up their eyes an' say, "Buddy, we're shet of you. We're gonna put a poor man in who'll do somethin' fer us."

But a lot o' things, the OEO money, I'm gettin' sick of it. They say they're gonna help the poor people. Then they get it all made up an' it's too much, we can't do nothin' fer you, you're not in the category. That's what they say. Let's not talk about helpin' people. If we're gonna help 'em, let's do somethin' about it. I've seed so many things that ain't right, I don't know what to do against it.

I think that the strip minin' coal industry has damaged Kentucky worse than anythin' I've ever seed. It's tore the beauty of the mountains up. And the poor man didn't get anythin' out of it. It went out to the big fellers. That's the way I see the strip mines. But coal mines has helped a lot. If it hadn't been fer some o' that in Clay County, the poor people would o' fared bad. They sure would. They had to work at somethin'. If they couldn't get the big price, they had to work at something to feed their families. But they worked many a day that they didn't get what pay they oughta have. They had to work at it. I've had to work at it; I've had to feed my young'uns. It was the only thing I could get to make any money at all. I could work out in the timber woods or somethin' like that, but I could make more money in the coal mines than I could that. But strip minin' has destroyed this country.

See, our road's tore up right here. And what did Goose Creek get out of this here strip mine? They never got one five cents off o' this. They should of had tax come off o' this went back to build some things. You know, we didn't get anythin' out of it. But that's the people lettin' 'em get away with it. If everybody'd walk up an' say, "Here!" an' our county officials went along, then we could collect it. We gotta have somebody down in them tax boards to say, "Here, buddy, you're takin' all this away from us." But these fellers an' them has always stood together.

It's like me. I ain't any richer now than when I was workin' in the coal mines. I had jest as much then. An' I haven't got any of it now, so how do you figure I could be any richer.

You know a lot of this land was leased way back on some kind of a broad form deed they talk about. And I've heard said that they didn't get nothin' fer it much. But their parents way back had done this, and there's nothin' I could do about it now 'lessen I lawed the broad form deed.

There's gonna have to be somethin' in East Kentucky besides coal mines. There's gonna have to be some jobs come in fer the young people. You take a feller fifteen years old right now. There's not gonna be any coal. There's not much coal here now in Clay County 'cept little bitty stuff. An' I ain't gonna work in it myself; I can't stand it.

I wouldn't advise none of my children to go into the coal mines, fer I don't want them to go through what I went through. I took one boy in. He got married when he wasn't too old. Well I took him in the mines, an' I had a time gettin' him out o' the mines. There wasn't nothin' else he could do here, but I didn't want him to go in. I said don't go. But he said I've got to work. And I agreed to take him *in the mines to work with me. I broke him in. I told him not to go and I'll tell the next boy not to go. Fer there's nothin' in the coal mines. You get the rock dust. You get the black lung. You work like a slave. No easy work in the coal mines.*

Young people they don't want to leave the state. They'd rather stay in Clay County or in Kentucky if there's jobs fer them to do. If they could get a job here an' make as much money . . . they'd come back to make a lot less money. But they go to Lexington. They go to Detroit. They go to Ohio. They go to Georgia. They go to Indianapolis, Indiana. Anywhere they can find work. They work at General Motors. They work at Ford's. And they work at regular jobs. A lot of these boys go off an' do construction. They work on the railroads. People out o' Goose Creek works on the railroads. Anybody who's got a high school education generally gets a job at a factory.

They don't see nothin' here right now. And they're young people. And they don't know what steps to take to get somethin' in here, to get shet o' politics an' get somethin' in here. I've talked to a lot of big people, an' they say, "You ain't got no roads in Clay County." If a business tries to start up here, I've heard said that they've said we don't need no business, but I don't know if that's true. Let me tell you somethin'. The reason they didn't want business here is they had a right smart o' coal work here at one time, an' they wanted these men to work in the coal mines fer them. And they knowed if there come a decent job here, that they're gonna quit an' go to it. An' these young men all stopped workin' in the coal mines an' left here. The coal operators in Clay County didn't want the WPA in here. They didn't want the Happy Pappies in here. They was mad. They say we can't hire a man to work in our coal mines. But they didn't care about the rock dust I was eatin' or the black lung I was gettin'. Let me go to heck; they're gonna hire another man the next day if they can get

*him. That's how I feel about it. They don't want these
gov'ment programs. They don't want these OEO programs.*

IV   The Mountain Community
   and the Outside World

There is only one true institution in the poor communities of Clay County, and that is the church. Though
church-going may not be the focal point of mountain life,
it is one of the few things that people do regularly and
together; and it is one of the few subjects about which
controversies arise that serve to split communities almost
irrevocably. There are many Protestant denominations in
Clay County—Brethren, Methodist, Pentecostal, Baptist,
Missionary Baptists, and others—and one small Catholic
church, and the differences or imagined differences of each
group in its practice of faith causes great consternation
among the rival sects. Methodists are accused of baptizing
children who are too young to understand the vows that
they take. Baptist churches argue among themselves about
dropping the old tokens of faith, like foot washing, from
their ceremonies. Pentecostals attack all others for deviating
from, or modernizing, the Bible. Congregations which
handle poisonous snakes look down upon those who do
not. And Catholicism is greatly feared by most mountain
Protestants—as it has been from the time men first left
European countries to venture to America. A good deal of
anti-Catholic feeling is vented in the more fundamentalist
Protestant churches, as is much anti-Semitism.

*We've got a few churches in this country that say they're
the only ones right. Some of 'em won't go to other churches,
which I disagree with that. You know they got 'nominations.
A Baptist, a Missionary, a United. You know Christ is the*

*head of the church. An' I don't care; a Missionary, a United
or somethin' like that is nothin'. That's jest a man-made
organization. Christ is the head of the church. It belongs to
him, an' he belongs to all o' the people. There's a lot o'
people in this country handle snakes. I don't believe in
that. I'm afraid o' rattlesnakes. There's some people handlin'
snakes in this country got bit an' died an' everythin' else.*

*We had one preacher preached down here said if you
didn't go to his church, you weren't nothin'; you were gone.
Everybody's gone if they didn't go to that church. An' I
quit goin' to it on account o' that. But he don't live
around here now. If you didn't go to his church you were
wrong. I've been there, an' I've heard him preach funerals.
An' he said, "Well, that brother or sister, he belonged to
this church, an' he's sure goin' to heaven." And I said,
buddy, you're jest a man yourself. You don't know where
she's goin' to, I said the Good Ol' Man above knows; not
you, preacher.*

But the various churches manage to coexist with one
another, and likely as many people attend some service as
do not. There is no great compulsion to go to a church. It
is frowned upon not to, more so for a woman than a man,
whose disinclination to endure an inactive two hours is
fairly well accepted. But most people enjoy church; it
offers the only real opportunity for neighbors to gather
together and for boys to meet girls. Most mountain churches
serve only small congregations which are generally from
the same community, and often made up of only three or
four extended families; this makes it more of a congenial
gathering. After services, people move on to neighbors'
homes to share dinner, which during the summertime can
be a fancy production. Often this will amount to a large
family get-together if sons and brothers have come back
from the city for the weekend.

Most country preachers are not seminary trained, but

simply men who have felt called upon to preach the gospel. Especially good preachers are widely competed for and are often called upon to preach revivals. In Clay and Knox counties, the Reverend Homer Jackson is a much acclaimed preacher, and the revivals which he leads generally pack the church. Preachers in the mountains are expected to preach, to be possessed with the Glory of God in the delivery of their sermons, and to transfer that fervor to their listeners. Methodist and Brethren ministers, who are mainly missionaries from the Midwest, sometimes have difficulty attracting followings because they are trained in a soft-spoken, reasoning style, in contrast with the loud, repetitive exhortations of the country Baptist. However, with the exception of the Pentecostals, once tagged "Holy Rollers," most mountain churches see less and less of the chanting and "shaking" by spirited listeners than they once did, and sermons are often directed at this distressing movement away from actual religious excitement.

There is much concern that people's faith, like the old rituals, is wasting away. The great sinners in the mountain religions are hypocrites, deceivers, selfish people, and Christians who debase their religion by turning from the old ways. To some, there is a much wider variety of sinners—men with long hair, women who cut their hair, people who play ball, young people who dance, and, of course, people who drink whiskey, which is to name just a few. Mountain religion dictates only one thing that must be done: accept Christ as the personal savior; outside of this, the beliefs of some sects are concerned mainly with the things not to be done, and the many sins that are so easy to commit. Above all else is the promise of heaven, where no one is troubled and no one is poor. Indeed, some hold the belief that poverty on this earth is in accord with God's plan and should not be complained of. When people do get somewhere in business, or land a good job, they, like thousands elsewhere, thank the "Ol' Man upstairs."

COMMUNITY GROUPS

In many communities throughout Clay County, the poor have gathered together to form community associations, neighborhood action councils, or improvement associations. These have been attacked by some preachers as being, among other things, communist, and they have been encouraged by as many more. County officials have done what they could to subvert these groups—from refusing community schools as meeting places to confiding their displeasure to all who would listen. In the main, the function of community organizations has been to see that available OEO and other government programs reach their communities and to mobilize people for various CAP affairs and area-wide meetings of the poor on such issues as black lung compensation legislation and the struggle for poor people's participation on the newly created Area Development District boards which, apparently, the Nixon administration hopes to use nationally to channel federal monies into areas lacking economic development. Much of the energy of these groups, as suggested previously, is invested in OEO-CAP programs. Three of the most highly organized community groups in the county were made "delegate agencies" by the CAP and given Head Start programs. Approximately one hundred children in the county attend Head Start.

Some of the community groups have succeeded in erecting buildings for centers, and some of them have begun to create small businesses using mostly the Self-Help program funds of the CAP. None has moved into areas like welfare rights, voter registration, or political activity, though OEO-sponsored groups and independent organizations in other mountain counties have, largely because these are not areas in which the CAP is involved. Community groups in Clay County did not come together to strike out at the forces which oppress them, as they did in the South. They were organized with the help of VISTA workers, Appalachian Volunteers, and the CAP staff to move against the physical manifestations of poverty—poor housing, no water systems, etc. This is clearly a far different approach than poor people in some other areas have taken, and one of the problems that it brings is that, with the gradual de-funding by OEO of the largest anti-poverty group in the mountains, the Appalachian Volunteers, and the general deflation of the CAP's power and budget over the last year or two, community groups in Clay County have been forced into a sort of lull in their activities.

Still, poor people's organizations continue to meet in the county, and people still look forward to the chance to come together and enjoy themselves talking. Some of the finest storytelling is heard among the men outside, and the choicest gossip is passed among the women; crops and weather are discussed, and occasionally, problems that confront the community are settled. And perhaps it is enough if an organization accomplishes these things.

Classes

There is a good deal of what might be called class aware-ness voiced in poor communities in the county. Towns-people are generally lumped together as the non-poor, controlling class, and, as noted before, no little antipathy is directed toward the doctors and lawyers, mine bosses, bankers, elected officials, and welfare and state employees —all of whom it is felt care nothing for the poor and, in fact, hope to keep the poor down. Some townsfolk do stress that they are not "country," and, as many of their young people grow up, they want nothing more than to go to an urban college or secretarial school and be considered worldly. It is quite likely that many people in town do not realize the extreme poverty in which others in their county live. Not knowing this makes more understandable the state-ments one hears about "those no-account hillbillies."

There are also two fairly distinct classes within the poor community: the working class and the welfare class. The mountaineers' view on welfare is rather mixed, and, of course, it is biased by whether he is, or is not, on public support. It is pretty much accepted that if a man needs help, he ought to have it. "Needs help" usually means "too sick to work." There is always the suspicion, however, that the man who does draw a check is not really unable to work, but, if that were actually the case, most would say of him that "he used his head," for while it is somewhat disapproved of not to work when able, it is a good sign if a man is clever. There are some men who would die before accepting welfare, either because they do not believe in "handouts" or because they do not want to undergo the considerable difficulty and humiliation involved in dealing with the welfare department. There are some people who look down on all welfare recipients, and many welfare recipients who take the reasonable view that they are just getting some of their tax dollars back and that it's nobody's business but their own. Everybody agrees that it is right to protect widows and orphans, but in the mountains many grown men draw a check, or have a medical card due to unemployment, or purchase food stamps. There is also the case of the disabled man, who for one of many possible reasons, cannot get approved for welfare, who cannot get a job, and who must keep up a home and family. The haggard, worn parents, the dirty, ill-clothed children, and the little one-room tar-paper-covered shack can make even his poor neighbors count their blessings. But often it will cause him to be spurned by his neighbors, as townspeople spurn the poor. Poor people are often insensitive to each other's problems, and in this sense, there is no compelling feeling of themselves as a class.

Well if they're sick, an' can prove that they're sick, they think it's a good thing. But I've heard a lot of people say, "I wish I could get on the welfare. I have to work." "The welfare, it ain't no 'count," they say. Which I think that they're wrong. I believe that the people ought to be honest. I don't know, but I've been told . . . I'm jest gonna tell you what I've been told . . . that you could go down there an' get on the welfare if you stood in the right corner. You could give the doctor somethin' an' he'd pass you, say you're bad off. But I think that the welfare's a good thing if people needs it an' are sick. They oughta have some income. But I don't think people oughta tell a lie or try to get something to get on welfare. If they can get jobs, I believe they oughta work fer it. I feel it's a good thing. I won't say nothin' about nobody that's on the welfare.

The workin' man, he knows he's a'gettin' his honest. He's a'workin' fer it. An' he knows his neighbor's gettin' it give to him. An' if he knows that his neighbor's gettin' his honest, an' is sick, then he's not gonna say nothin' about it. But if he feels that he's tricked 'long the line somewhere, he'll say he oughta be workin'. If I knowed that my neighbor right out yonder was on the welfare, an' me a' workin' eight hours a day in the coal mines, an' if he had got that without bein' sick, then I don't think he ought to have it. But if he is sick, I'd feel good about it. And I think everybody else feels jest about the same way.

I know that there's a lot o' these kids that needs somethin' bad. And I feel that there's a lot of people that ought to be on the welfare. I don't know no man's feelin's. Nor I don't want to say nothin' agin him no way. You know I might have to get on welfare myself some day. And they're gonna say the same thing about me that I said. If you're sick, you oughta have the welfare. You know, I'm no doctor, an' if a doctor OK's a man, he ought to be an honest man. He ought to do the straight business. But I've heard people say that there's people on welfare who oughtn't to be. I don't know. I know there's people, I don't know what their trouble is, but they look like they need somethin'.

I feel that the poor man can't help himself. An' that's

*what's wrong with the world today. They're lookin' down on
that poor man place o' helpin' him. If the people had somethin' to help that man in Granny's Branch, or ever where he
lives, I think that they'd be a'doin' a better thing than
they're doin'. I think that they're a'punchin' that man down
when they oughta be a'givin' him somethin'. As long as we
talk about our neighbors an' say he's too poor fer us to fel-
lowship with, if we're up above that man a little bit an' can
lend a helpin' hand to that man, we oughta be a'doin' it.
An' that's what's the matter with the world today.*

*You know I don't have any money much myself, but if
I seed a man like that an' lived close to that man, an' if he
needed five dollars, I'd give him five dollars in money or
somethin' jest as free as I could. If he'll try to help hisself. An' he's a sick man. But if a man jest sits down, I mean
if he ain't no account . . . . But I don't know, you see. I
think the man's sick jest to look at him. Or somethin's
wrong with him. I don't know what it is. But you know
they got a lot o' people in the world today is sick people,
an' the people needs to be a'helpin' them people. An' that's
one thing that's the matter with the people today. They
don't help one another much.*

THE MOUNTAIN PERSONALITY

Mountain people are often characterized as being independent. Perhaps the nature of that independence bears
examining here. It does not strictly mean that mountain
people refuse to follow any but their own lead. More truly
it means that they do not like to be told what to do; they
do not like to bend to the will of the majority; they
do not like people such as county officials, sheriffs, congress-
men, presidents, game wardens, etc.; they do not like people
who deny their own nature, e.g., wear a tie; they don't
think the idea of "working together" is a requisite for getting things done; they believe in settling their own disputes;

they think they're tougher, but also friendlier, than most other people. Much has been made of this attribute of independence by those who extol "traditional American virtues," and it has been much lamented by outsiders intent on organizing mountain communities or serving the mountain poor. They are not very easy to serve, for they even have a hard time getting along with themselves, except within their own family structures. The well-understood need to go one's own way often comes in conflict with the rigid codes of conduct laid down by church and custom, and men and women find themselves chastised by their neighbors for this or that breach of unwritten, or maybe biblical, law. Within the confines of the little mountain settlements, grievances are not soon forgotten but tend to break into small-scale feuds that sometimes end in shootings or trips to the penitentiary.

They think too much agin their neighbors. I think that is one thing that is ruinin' the world today, that they don't share their loads with one another, their burdens with one another enough. They look on another feller, they might think he's got a little more'n he has, they'll try to knock him out o' somethin'. That's wrong. I don't care what somebody else has got; I'm not gonna try to knock him out o' nothin'. I don't know how you get that out o' people. But you know that's true. They're agin their neighbors; they talk about their neighbors an' say, "There's nothin' to that feller," an' all such as that. I call it selfish. I think that that keeps 'em down a lot o' times. I think that that's one of our problems. I've tried to tell people to fergit about such as that and do somethin' to help somebody because holdin' a grudge, old grudges . . . lot o' people got old grudges against one another, an' they'll die with that in 'em. You know I think that you've got to forgive people. If I had anythin' agin you, I'd come right out an' tell you. I don't believe in gettin' out all over the country an' talkin' about it. If I got somethin' agin you

*right now, or you done somethin' I don't like, place o' me
a'goin' up an' down this road a'sayin' you done somethin', I
oughta go to you an' tell you an' say you ought not do that
no more. An' that stops it right there. But if I go tellin' it to
my neighbors, an' they go tellin' it outside, it don't get no
smaller, it gets bigger everytime it's told.*

*You should not fight your neighbors; I never have tried
to fight nobody. An' I didn't see that I could fight people an'
live. It's people today who'll tell anythin' in the world, an'
try to down you. Sometime I get nervous, but I've had
persecutin' all my life. That doesn't hurt me. I've done a
lot o' things that I'm glad of, an' I don't care fer nobody
a'talkin' about me. But now if you've never got people to
talk about you, you've never done nothin'. When you find
a man that nobody never speaks nothin' of, you say, well
that man never did nothin' no way. You can't have people
talk good about you all the time.*

The mountain man is quick to anger, and in return for
some offenses against him, he is expected to mete out his
own punishments. A man must guard his own property,
and disputes about ownership of stock or dogs can provoke
lengthy gun battles along the moonlit, winding roadways.
Young men do not take lightly the idea of courting a girl
in another settlement or "across the hill." He knows he
might have to fight it out with her neighboring suitors.
Should he mistreat the girl, he might be ambushed on
the darkened roads by her brothers. There is no crime worse
than adultery or ill-treatment of another's wife. It is expected of the aggrieved husband that he will kill the offender, and for this reason men go out of their way to show
no signs of interest in each other's wives. That mountaineers
strive vigorously to settle their scores is shown by the fact
that in Clay County there is a shooting or other violent
crime on the average of about once a month.

Usually, people have little use for the law. They prefer to

settle their differences in their own way. When a sheriff is summoned to settle a complaint, it is most often a woman, not a man, who has called him. Few are the men who have not spent a night in jail or paid a fine, but sheriff's deputies are not overly anxious to take in men because the men often put up a good fight before they go.

On summer days, men like to go squirrel hunting which, like fishing, is mostly an art of sitting still waiting for something to move. The Clay County game warden is kept busy stalking up steep mountainsides trying to locate the roaring shotgun blasts of an out-of-season hunt. On fall nights, men loose their dogs to track down the big coon that less and less roam the forests. A good hunter is as highly regarded as a good mechanic, and a good coon dog is more highly regarded than just about anything else.

Dogs, hunting rifles, and knives are continually being traded in the informal markets of downtown street corners and country general stores. Some claim to make their living by alternately trading and selling. The true trader deals in the "antique"—the World War II high-powered automatic, old "Case" brand knives, or "Old Timers" without the USA on the blade—and men might travel miles to find the owner of such a gem. It is no small gift when a father passes on to his son a 1918 officer's pistol.

A time-honored mountain profession not as yet mentioned is moonshining. In a county that has optioned "dry," such as Clay, there is a considerable demand for good homemade whiskey. Pure corn liquor is a virtual myth to the moonshine drinker, as it is extremely expensive to make and generally substituted for by much diluted mixtures, and it is heard about only once every few years in a given county when a moonshiner, moved by sheer benevolence, runs off a small batch for his best customers and friends. The moonshiner is a well-known figure in most communities, but he, unlike the bootlegger who sells beer at fifty cents a can, is left fairly unmolested by county law officers.

There is also in the mountain character a lot of simple country goodness. The usual parting words between people are, "Stay with us; spend the night," "Gotta go, y'all come with us," and people are not usually put out if you take them up on their offer. Anyone visiting a home at mealtime is expected to stay for dinner. People do not mind stopping on the road to help each other with car troubles. Work like "robbing" bee gums (so called because farmers traditionally raised bees in hollowed sections of gum trees rather than in manufactured hives), fixing tractors, and loading trucks is shared without comment. But picking beans, canning, and hoeing fields, which were once community efforts where all who could joined in, going from house to house, are now jobs you must pay others to help you with. This lost magic of working together is often talked about and wondered at by mountain people, and no one seems to know why it is no longer there, except, "people stopped doin' it." It is speculated that the World War, or maybe welfare, had something to do with it, but to no one is the connection quite plain.

RELATIONS TO OUTSIDERS AND THE MODERN WORLD

The mountains of Kentucky, which for many decades were little visited or heard about by people elsewhere, have seen their share of outsiders in the last few years. They, in the persons of anti-poverty workers, community organizers, and government men from Frankfort or Washington, are generally met fairly, if with some curiosity and aloofness— though the outsider, with his peculiar dress, manner, speech, and ideas, sticks out like a sore thumb. People are usually willing to listen to what an outsider has to say, and often they are willing to be dominated by his decisions, for he represents all that people have been taught is better than themselves—the urban born, the educated, and the sophisticated. Of course there are some who will speak bitterly about "all those people comin' in here tryin' to civilize us," and often outsiders will arouse scornful criticism by openly violating what is considered proper conduct between the sexes, by admitting to a disbelief in God, or by talking about the draft and the war.

From time to time preachers or small businessmen will begin to worry about communists and do a good bit of talking about these "strange foreigners," but for the most part poor people put the outsider into one of two categories: the suspect, not to be fully trusted; or the benevolent protector who will fight off welfare departments and school systems. Regardless of which group he falls into, the outsider is not really approved of. This is because most outsiders come to the mountains with the desire to help, in an obvious way, and most mountain people, much as they want to see justice done them, vaguely resent the idea of being helped. For all this, there comes an occasional outside organizer who can quickly adjust to a new people and be accepted by them and quietly draw people together. Yet any outsider, by his presence, serves as proof that the people where he comes from, the people in the towns and cities, do not need help, that, somehow, they have made it.

I'll tell you, I guess that outside people is all right. I've seen a lot of outside people myself, an' it takes a outside person who comes in here a long time to get used to how the mountain people lives. I can see where they can do a lot o' good things, but they got to get used to the people before they can do anything. I think outside people's been a lot o' help to us. Course, you know, a lot o' people, when they come in here, they say, "Well, maybe they're spies, or communists, or somethin' like that," which is wrong.

We live diff'rent here than they do in the cities. You know we have outside . . . houses. We don't have like they do in the cities. An' actually we eat diff'rent, I guess. I guess you do know that. We raise what we eat here mostly. That's hard fer people to get used to . . . . You jest can't come in this place right here an' people take up with you right now in a few days. You got to stay around till people learns you before they'll pay too much attention to you.

If you go up this branch right here this evenin', you're a strange man, they want to know what you're up here fer. An' if you come in here like a VISTA. . . . They say they're comin' up here to, you could say, organize or to help the people. But I've never seen any of 'em come up here right off the reel an' know plumb blank what they was comin' up here fer. I can't go in a place, not knowin' what I'm a' goin' fer an' tell the people what I'm about. Now it looks to me if I go in a strange place in this country or anywheres they got to find out what I'm doin' in there an' pretty quick. And that's the way the VISTA's are, or anybody else. They want to know what you're here for, an' you've got to tell them what you're here for. Of course, it's nobody here that I know of that'd have anythin' agin people, but they jest don't understand what they're here for. I feel that VISTA's supposed to be here to help people. What I mean to help people, to get people to help themselves. I believe in people tryin' to do somethin' to help themselves. Until they do, I don't see much.

They's plenty of 'em comes down, they don't know what they're doin'. Yes sir, there's plenty of 'em comes here don't know. If you go up in these hollers to work with these people, you got to have somethin' to tell these people. If you jest go up there an' talk about organizin' people, well that's all right, but people gonna ask you directly what you're gonna organize them for. I'm gonna have to tell these people what kind o' resource I'm gonna give 'em. To help these people so they can help themselves.

It's not too many people in this country worry about communists. It's a lot o' things goes around if you're a outside man. You got some people in this country'll say that's communist. Well I don't believe in callin' people communist

*until I know who they are. I don't think there's been any
communists around this area here. You know they've heard
talk o' Russia, an' it's been said to me long back that, you
know Russia's communist people, that they're gonna come
in here an' they're gonna do this an' that. If you was an
outside person, why I could ruin you here, buddy. I could
say you're a communist, and, brother, you wouldn't do no
more good here. I could kill you in Goose Creek in three
days if I wanted to. I could go an' say you're nary a thing
but a communist, and boy they'd be through with you then.
They'd say, we'd better not fool with him.*

*I know of some outsiders who's caused some troubles
back in Otter Creek, but that's over with now. There was a
girl who made some mistakes. A girl can't come in this
country and know right from the start . . . well, you
gotta know how to act. I had a girl in Otter Creek, an' she
made some bad mistakes, and it's not out o' some people yet.*

Q. Are there any rules that you'd make for an outsider
coming here to organize?

*Well, if it was a girl come in here, I'd lay down a rule
that they should not be out with men after dark. And they
should wear their clothes more decently, a lot o' times. Like
shorts an' things like that, in this country, don't work. It
ain't right, but a lot o' old people an' a lot o' other people
talks about 'em. You know, it ain't none o' my business what
other people wears. But I know what the people says. But
you know we watch people. We talk about their dress bein'
too short. Up to here, you know, up to 'round here. Jesus
Christ. That's right.*

The mountain people feel a deep wonder at the outside
world that makes the news and builds the machines and
steals away their young. Some of the feeling is that things
have gotten out of their hands, and that their lives are being
directed from Washington, Detroit, and Cincinnati. It

seems that all that is important is being done in the cities,
and that they, far up the mountain back roads, are no longer
a part of what America has come to be. The things that
go on in the cities do not please the mountain people. They
hear of riots and hoodlums and painted women, beer joints
and slums, and neighbors you never meet. The cities seem a
terrible place where anyone can get mugged on the street, or
have his wallet stolen, and where you must carry a gun in
your car. The fact that so many of their sons and daughters
have moved there increases the worry.

*Well, it's a lot diff'rent from here, the cities. They live
diff'rent. An' a lot o' people have never been in the cities
too much. Some of 'em has. They live diff'rent ways. They
seem to be crowded up more. An' I don't like the city myself
to live in. But I don't have no kin to people in the cities.*

*I don't like to stay right in a crowded up place. I've been
all over the cities. I jest don't like to get there an' jest sit
down on the porch an' sit there. An' in the cities I've been,
I don't see them visitin' people too much. I don't know.
I don't like to go down to Manchester an' stay there fer
over an hour. Long as I can get out o' that town. I want
out. Now that's the way I see it. Which I got nothin' agin
nobody in the cities. I jest don't like a town, not any crowded
up place. I want to get away from it.*

*Drinkin' an' gamblin' is very bad in the cities. I mean
they say. I never seed much of it. You know you can go
anywheres they got beer an' whiskey, an' they go on more,
an' they have more goin's on than we do here. We don't
have no whiskey in Clay County. We have plenty of it, too,
but it's not legal; they bootleg it.*

*I wouldn't say that people thinks they're an evil place.
I've heard people say that there's a lot o' meanness goes on
in a city, but I don't know. See I know we got mean people
anywheres we go, but I wouldn't want to say the cities,
like Manchester, was an evil place. I can't judge people.*

There is a strong sense in mountain communities that the world is turning into a very evil place, and that all of these modern things, which are so hard to grasp, are very wrong. Movies, dancing, television, and other entertainments are considered by many to be "the devil's work," and to see them enjoyed so widely in the cities and accepted by the young people in the mountains makes the whole modern tide seem unholy. Much of the preaching heard in mountain churches concerns the way in which the world is turning away from Christ. Even those who sit and watch the news on their televisions become greatly fearful about what is happening in "modern America," and what they have come to know will dominate their future.

They don't like that modern stuff. They say that's what's ruinin' the world today. It's modern stuff. I think, jest to tell you the truth about it, that a lot o' people don't want to go in the cities. For they can't dress . . . that big tie an' that suit. An' away from here, in the cities, you got to dress pretty well or they won't let you eat in the restaurant, unless you got a big tie. I've heared it said that you have to have on the right kind of suit or they won't look at you. An' that's one reason that a lot o' people don't like the cities. You know the way people dresses in the cities, we can't afford it here. These poor mountain people can't. They're not able to get that kind o' suit. They don't have no jobs to buy the clothes with. An' they never been away too much, an' that's what they think about it. They say that's too modern fer us. We don't want in that place.

There's some people in Goose Creek don't believe in a television. They say if you got a television it's wrong. They show some movies on the television, an' things like that, an' they say it's wrong to look at that. That you should not be a'lookin' at movies.

Well, I don't think it's wrong. I think the TV is a good thing. What I think about it, it's a lot o' trainin', a lot o' experience. An' they can't prove to me it's wrong. If I had a TV an' I didn't go to church or do somethin' but watch that TV, or wouldn't turn my hand to help people that needed it. I'd say then I'm a'doin' wrong. But I got a TV up here, an' if anythin' comes on I don't want to watch it's got a knob there I can turn off. An' I got a conscience that teaches me when I do wrong or steal or anythin' else, but not about a TV.

If you got a TV, I don't know if they think too bad about you, but they might say, "That feller might do anythin'," if he had a TV. Which I've got one, an' I'm gonna keep it till I'm ready to get shet of it. I think this is a free world an' a free America, an' I think every individual's got a right to his own beliefs, an' that's the way I'm gonna believe it. An' if you can cite me any diff'rences, I'm not gonna fall out with you, but I might get shet of you.

There's some women here, if they went to the city, they'd say that the very devil's right here. She'd see the women with the short dresses on, shorts, an' then she might see some o' that beer an' stuff that they got in them joints. She's say, "Lordy Mercy, the world's gonna end right now." She'd see long hair. She'd say, "That's nary a thing but the devil; them's them hippies." That's right. Better not let your hair get long around here.

You can't do no good in this country with long hair. Lot o' people would talk about you wearin' a long hairdo. They say that the Bible says that a woman's hair is her glory, and a man's hair . . . I forget how the Bible says it, but anyway, they want a man to have short hair.

The moon landing in 1969, which so inspired men elsewhere, was largely upsetting in mountain communities. Very few people believed that men actually had done what the government said they had done, and many of those who did believe it doubted that it was a right thing to do. Many declared, before the landing took place, that God would prevent it, quoting scriptures that said God placed the moon in the heavens to give light and arguing that man should not try to change what God has arranged and that living men could not enter heaven. After the news of the successful landing was broadcast, many shook their heads and called it a fake, and from the pulpits of not a few churches it was called "the great deceit" and part of the ascendancy of hypocrites and sinners to power, part of what is going wrong in the world today. Many people, it is sure, saw in the triumphant speeches and parades after the moon shot a very important step being taken by the world towards evil and evil modern ways, and away from the truer, more trustworthy path that has led poor people in the mountains through lives of greater hardship and suffering than many of our modern people would like to think about.

Well, they said he didn't go. Several people said he didn't go. I was asked that yesterday; the preacher asked me that yesterday. He ate dinner with me, and he'd heard about it, an' he asked me did I believe the man went to the moon. An' my daddy-in-law was up there. An' I said I believed the man went to the moon. I'll tell you the reason I believe it. I told him that I don't believe the government, the federal government, would get on the microphone an' talk to the people an' try to deceive the people like that. I believe he went to the moon, and I believe he walked on it. Ed was sittin' right there. I don't believe Ed thinks they went to the moon. I said the reason I think that, preacher, is that the Lord give man the knowledge to make the thing, an' if it hadn't been His will to go there, we would not o' went there. An' I said, I'm believin' he went, an' I looked right at him. An' the preacher said, "I guess you're right." An' Ed never would say too much. Ed said that they could take a picture of anythin' an' show it to people.

Some people feels that the Lord put the moon up there, an' He put it up there to give light. Not for people to fool with. That's what some o' them people says. But you know I feel, goin' to the moon, we wasn't tryin' to do nothin' to the moon to hurt nothin'. And that's the reason that I believe that we went to the moon. A lot of people, you know, don't believe that the moon is as big as this whole earth. A lot of people thinks that the moon is jest that little light that you see. That's what Ed believes about it. "The moon's as big as this whole earth, Ed," I said. "No," he said, "not nearly." Well I couldn't afford to argue with him.

I believe that we beat Russia to the moon, an' I believe that we're the sharpest nation in the world, an' I believe we went to the moon, an' I don't know, we might go further. I'm very proud o' them men a'goin' there. Well, we need the money down here. We need the money. But that showed Russia that they wasn't the smartest nation in the world. It took a lot o' money to get to the moon, but you don't know, that could help bring peace quicker'n' anythin' in the world. I've studied about that. But you know that the poor people needed some money down here. Maybe we'll have money to do that job an' this one too. I don't know whether we can do that, but we can solve this thing jest as soon as people get together an' go to doin' things to get money. I've had to work all my life, an' I've raised eight kids. I've worked for fifty cents a day, an' I never did starve. Now I don't have too much, but I think if the people will try to do things, we can get something to do here.

V   The Past and the Future

People look back on times past in the mountains with longing. They are remembered as days when there was plenty of good timber on the hillsides, when there was big coal to be mined, when meal and flour and lard could be bought cheap, and when young men and women would settle down close by and raise big families. It is a tragic, and by no means necessary, thing that all of this is gone now. Wiser men might have looked ahead and seen that no good comes from methodically pillaging a region, building for its people no industries for the future, and allotting them no place in the fantastic growth of America. For now the mountains are as they were first conceived by the mining corporations—large mounds of rocky dirt surrounding tiny valleys of worn-out soil—except that now there is no longer the timber that once could be seen covering every mountaintop. A land of poorly educated, hard working, but tired-out people. Why was big business so hasty about removing the coal? Surely there was a better way to do it—a way that would not cause the miner to say, "The thing that's wrong with this coal business is a few men gets it all, an' the rest of us is jest slaves."

It's been a change in livin' the last twenty, thirty years, a lot. Way back, you see, we made what we got. When I was growing up myself, we didn't go to stores for things. We made it on the farm. An' the farms is wore out, an' the hillsides is washed away. Of course wages got higher, an' the people stepped up from what they was. They couldn't live now like they used to live. If I had to back up in these mountains, it's all right maybe, but like we used to farm, ten hours a day from six till five in the evenin', we couldn't live. The mountains won't make it. An' they got more jobs, a lot more jobs. But it's not enough jobs. They have more people now than they used to be here. It's stepped up so high, is one thing. Costs is got so high. People have to pay more, an' they have to get money fer other things. They haven't nothing to get on by.

They used to pick beans. They used to farm. They used to swap o' work. If a man's fields got weedy, they went out an' hoed it out. That's the past about it. Now they won't, but you know there's not too many people around here farms to do that. I think if I needed accommodation, I think the people around here would do that. I don't know about money. Used to they did without money. I remember way back, my daddy he took sick one summer, an' he never was in the hospital but once or twice that I knowed of in his life, an' we had a great big field of corn yonder. I wasn't grown. An' the people came in an' hoed that out. The weeds was knee high.

It's been a lot o' diff'rence. Used to we went to church, an' we rid a mule. I've seed 'em hitched up all day. I mean they rid five or six miles to church. An' now they got automobiles to ride, an' nine times outa ten, place o' goin' to church they go to a drive-in or somewheres else. And when they had to ride their mules, they went to church. They had 'em standin' underneath the shade trees. I've seen forty, fifty mules standin' out from that church on Mill Creek down by that schoolhouse. Hitched all over that hill in the bottoms. They'd ride five or ten miles. Now, they got a car, an' they go other places.

What the future holds for the mountains of Kentucky seems quite bleak. Eventually enough industry may move in to employ the bulk of those who have not by that time left. What will happen to those who cannot or will not leave for the city, who cannot wait for a job fifteen years from now, or who will be too old, unschooled, or unskilled to get a job if ever they are plentiful—this is a question that no one has answered. Presumably these people, who number in the thousands in each mountain county of the state, will be left to scratch out a living as best they can, to grovel for food stamps, and to die. If this is what does happen, much that is beautiful will die with them. A large part of America will die. That mountain culture with its proud people, its beautiful gospel hymns, its fierce religion—it will be gone. A people as distinct from others as are the southern white, southern black, American Indian, or Mexican-American will have been erased. And that part of the American litany which calls for human dignity and the general welfare of man will have held itself up to be called worthless again.

It should be noted that the triumph of one generation can burden the next. The Tennessee Valley Authority, a monument to the New Deal, through displacing hundreds of families, served to create cheap electric power for the mountains and the South where there had been no power before. It opened the way over large areas for the coming and the growth of industry.

By far, the greatest users of the TVA's incredible output today are government military installations, principally the atomic research complex at Oak Ridge, Tennessee. One source of Oak Ridge's power is a TVA steam plant which sends virtually all its current to Oak Ridge. The steam that produces the electricity is created by the speedy burning of low-grade coal from the mountains of Kentucky. The purchaser of over 20 per cent of the strip mine coal from the mountains of Kentucky is the Tennessee Valley Authority.

The great pride we feel, and the major interest we have in the development of inexpensive power, need to be re-evaluated in light of the fact that we currently sponsor the annual destruction of thousands of mountain acres, and that we are in conflict with the needs and hopes of poor people in the Kentucky mountains.

The mountains have been made so much as the target area for the War on Poverty that now its many planners and its shrinking population have become somewhat battle weary. The poverty war partly succeeded in achieving the goals of its many projects, but it failed to dent, much less eradicate, the poverty of this region. Too little money—and certainly too little thought—was given to the fight. Appalachia stands as testimony to the many blunders of our American system. These are not to be corrected by the investment of a few million dollars spread across an area of such size; too much damage has been done for that.

The mountains have been carelessly and wantonly ravaged during this century. Billions of tons of coal have been removed at an enormous expense in lives and hardship. Not one ton had taxes levied upon it to enrich the counties from which it came. Not one miner shared in the profits of the coal companies. Surface mining in eastern Kentucky has done violent harm to the beauty of the mountains, has polluted and deadened creeks, and has left scars that only serious land reclamation, not time, could ever heal. The coal industry gave jobs, but no roads were built from the profits of the coal, for coal is moved by rugged trucks along main highways and by rail cars. The coal industry spawned no economic development because, aside from machines and trucks, it requires no secondary industry to supply its needs. Business did not follow the coal companies because miners' wages were too low to encourage buying. Water systems were not built because mines need no water. Waste removal systems were not created because rock and slag could be dumped down the mountainside or piled up in valleys. No power lines were laid because mines can more cheaply use generators. The coal industry could come and go, leaving nothing behind it.

Yet the industry has not gone; only that part of it which offered plentiful jobs. In 1968, more than 100,000,000 tons of coal were taken from Kentucky, a record total. Close to half of this was taken from the flat land of western Kentucky where mechanized operation is much easier to employ. More and more small mines were shut down, leaving more otherwise unskilled coal miners unemployed. A rise was seen in the number of large underground mines, the sort in which horrible disasters have occurred—like the one in Farmington, West Virginia, where seventy-eight men were killed by a gas explosion.

The mountains still hold plenty of coal; what they do not have are enough jobs to go around. Resentment against this state of affairs flared openly during the still smoldering anti-strip mine fight. And hopefully the miners' anger will continue to make itself heard. A great debt is owed Kentucky and the people who live there. They have not only surrendered the mineral that once gave their region hope of prosperity, but they have given of themselves, as laborers in a killing occupation. That debt will not be repaid by inviting industry to the mountains—that would follow the pattern set forth by big coal: industry that will destroy land, take without giving, and pay only as high a wage as is needed to ensure an "abundant labor supply."

The debt could only be repaid by diverting what is left of Appalachian coal to the benefit of the region, toward building roads and schools; by returning, through government, some of what has been taken to promote industry owned and run by mountain people; by halting the destruction of mountain lands with surface mining; and by paying heed to the voices that can be heard in the mountains— voices of poor people who have seen for themselves the worst that America can do and who have more hope than most groups that our society can be reshaped to the benefit of all.

I imagine there's a lot o' people yet who's never got on their feet from the Depression. You take a lot o' people in Clay County; they've got no money to make money with. An' they can't get out. You take you jest barely gettin' enough money to get by with; if you ain't got a job that you can make a little money with, to lay it up to make money with, you always stay poor.

You take the people on the welfare; they jest barely got enough money to live on, an' they owe their check jest as quick as they get it to some store down here. Well, they take that check an' give it to that store; they live one month on the credit. They ain't got $50 or $100 ahead that they could go out an' buy somethin' that they knowed they could make $25 or $30 with.

I call that pretty poor myself. An' there's plenty of 'em in Clay County today. And until they got that broke, they'll stay poor. Now I've been here long enough to know that. And I've actually been that way myself. You know if you work fer the coal mines all week, an' you make $75, or $300 a month, you can owe a lot o' debt. I've been in debt 16, $1800 at one time. Well by the time I paid that an' run my family, I didn't have no money to make nothin' else with. I had to pay these debts. An' that's the reason that today you ain't makin' enough money. You're jest makin' enough to pay your debts an' sort o' breathe by, not livin' like you oughta live, an' send your young'uns to school. You had to be mighty careful to do that. Now buddy that's true.

I believe in payin' anybody for their work, but we got a lot o' things that some people can ᵔake 'em $10,000 a year. An' I pay as much tax as them $10,000 a year men on one job. I don't think that anybody ought to have big money. I don't think they ought to have 12, $15,000 a year an' a poor man down here gettin' maybe $3,000. That's what's the matter with the world. All the big men's got all the money, an' the poor man ain't got nothin'. I don't know if that sounds right or not, but that's the way I see it.

I can tell the truth. I've worked all my life. From a boy up. You know, I guess I done as much work as anybody. It's not been easy work; it's been hard work. It's been with a shovel. It's been with a cross-cut saw. It's been workin' in stave woods. It's been workin' in a saw mill. I've cut trees with a cross-cut saw. They got power saws now; we didn't have a power saw. Comin' from the coal mines, I'd have to scoot fifty feet off a hill, couldn't walk. Do you believe that? My legs hurt me so bad in the calves of my legs I jest couldn't make the next step. I got out an' scooted off they was so sore. But that was when I started work in the coal mines. I said I'll never stand this. But I did stand it. I got used to it.

VI Remarks on the Changing Times

Well, I could see a change in the people. I could see a change in the land. You know, back twenty years ago, we had plenty timber in this country. It was plenty timber work. You could get a job. Well, that timber's all gone now. And people's got to look fer somethin' besides timber fer a job. And one way people has changed from what they was twenty years ago, they've learned a lot more things about a lot o' things than they used to know. I'd say thirty or forty years ago, if they went to Manchester they rode a mule. They didn't know what was goin' on up in Manchester then; they thought that was somethin'. Now when they go, they go in a car. They go faster. They don't ride a mule. And they've caught on to the racket some. They know what's goin' on.

I've rid a mule from right here on Mill Creek into Manchester. Since the cars have come along, they've quit the mules and they've changed. They learned a lot more about the world than they knowed twenty or thirty years ago. I can see a lot o' changes in everythin'. There's a lot o' poor people yet. Nobody wants to up an' own that they're poor. They're tryin' to hold their heads up, but they are poor. You know it used to be big chestnut oak, white oak, that they made staves out of. That's all gone now. And you have to look to somethin' else fer a job.

I would say it's changed from what it used to be. One way, if it's carried out, we got stricter laws than there used to be over the mine system. Used to, you would have an inspector . . . you've got 'em now, but they are a little bit harder than they used to be. But they're not hard enough.

In places it's worser. Used to be, you wouldn't ride down these roads an' see the whole top of a mountain slipped off. That was all there in timber. An' where's that at? I think a lot of it's they took the coal out an' 'stroyed the young timber, and hurt somebody and made their earth poorer. For the young generation. And the coal didn't do a lot o' poor people any good. Helped the big man, but not the worker. I can see on Mill Creek, there's a whole lot of level land up there, I can see, if time keeps on another twenty, thirty years an' people increases like they are, I can see that full o' houses up there.

I don't know. I can see it may be a tough place, if nothin' comes in diff'rent. I can see, I guess I shouldn't say it, people gettin' weaker. We live in a world right now that, I don't know how to say it, but I think ther'll have to be somethin' done to make our state a better place to live in. We got a lot o' young people who's comin' up, an' they're comin' up wrong. I don't know if you agree with me or not. I don't think they're teachin' 'em too good. I think that they should teach 'em to treat everybody alike when they come up, an' not have a group o' people sayin', "Oh, there's nothin' to that man. There's nothin' to that woman." That's no way to raise kids. They ought to be raised to treat everybody alike, an' I believe we'd have a better world to live in. That might sound foolish to you.

Our people today is wantin' you to give 'em somethin'. Now that's a pretty bad thing to say, but I'm tellin' the truth. They've been that way fer a long time. We have a community meetin' right here, an' they can have forty or fifty people. And you sit right here an' ask 'em what they want to do, an' they'll sit right up there an' wait fer you to come up with the answer. If I knowed somethin' I could get fer people to help 'em, then I oughta get that. But I think that there ought to be a group o' people start talkin' about what they want to do. Long as you sit right where you are and depend on someone else doin' it for you, you ain't gonna do no good.

You've heard talk of welfare. You've heard talk of com-

modity. You've heard talk of food stamps. You heard talk of OEO programs, which I'll say ain't got down to where they oughta been. But they think there's a lot o' money they can get. Now it's gonna take people to get these people doin' jobs. They're gonna have to go around. They're gonna have to sit on their porches. They gotta tell 'em what they could do, an' try to get these people learnt to go to talkin' . . . organizing.

That's the worst thing that I ever done was to promise a man that I was gonna do somethin' an' I can't do that. That's a'killin' me right there. They'll say that man promised me somethin' an' now he let me down.

And another thing that makes it bad. You take all these diff'rent churches, diff'rent 'nominations, and they'll say that they are the best people. The United Missionary or Holiness or what have you, we're the people that's right. They're wrong. I don't think that 'nominations mean anythin'. They're jest mountain folk. We got a lot o' preachers that need straightenin' out. They oughta preach the Bible, an' quit talkin' about 'nominations.

The CAP's have done some things to bring people together, and they've done some things to draw 'em away. They've done some things, an' they've hurt too. They have brought some people together, I'll state that, but they've brought not enough people together. Nothin' like it. They've not done what they oughta do to bring people together.

The Mountains and the South

COMPARISON TO THE SITUATION OF SOUTHERN BLACKS

Much can be said in comparing the situations of the poor blacks in the Mississippi Delta and the poor whites in the mountains of Kentucky. Here an attempt is made only to illustrate certain areas of similarities and differences.

The rich, flat, burning land of the Mississippi Delta yielded naturally to the development of huge, many-thousand-acre plantations. In such earth, agricultural industry can grow, and cotton, a nation-building crop, was well suited to the Delta. It was for the sake of cotton, and of the great farming empires, that the black man was brought to work the land. Little has happened to change the positions of rich white landowner, impoverished black worker, and struggling small farmer. When the plantation aristocracy decided to mechanize their farms, it wreaked spectacular havoc throughout the whole system. The black tenant farmers and sharecroppers had nothing of their own to fall back on, no alternate sources of employment, no land, no history of diverse occupation. The particularly terrible conditions that prevail in the Delta today are blamable on the too long unchallenged life of the plantation system. With each man's job, income, home, and all the political power held in the hand of the plantation owner, it is impossible to expect a rising out of poverty. A family cannot even repair its own home because there is no money and because the home is not its own to repair. A family cannot build another, because there is no money and because it owns no land to put a house on. A powerless people deprived of the right to produce has no choice but to make the best of poverty— a poverty unparalleled in this country today—or to strike out against the collection of forces that hold them bound— an alternative that is being taken more and more often in the cities where the southern family has found more subtle and complex barriers to a decent life.

The political and economic systems developed quite differently in the mountains of Kentucky. The men who settled the mountains came to make a living and a new life, not to make money. There was no question of industry, agricultural or otherwise. Men hunted, farmed, and built what they could to support themselves. It was not until the coal industry moved in at the turn of the century that any real change took place, and even then, except near the big mechanized mines where sprawling coal camps were erected, most men farmed or kept a little farm going while they worked in the mines. The operators of the large-scale, northern-owned coal companies controlled the politics and the police of the principal mining counties—Harlan, Perry, and others—and theirs was a regime so bitter that it provoked the bloody union battles in the state. The power of the coal barons was never complete in the outlying coal counties, like Clay, where most of the mines were small, "shovel" mines that were owned by mountain interests, if not locally. In these counties, few men came rich or got rich. The ones who ran things were more successful businessmen and farmers who were not so far in stature above the poor man himself. Miners and other laborers, for the most part, retained ownership of their land and did not forsake it for the lure of the coal camp where the good wage was coupled with exorbitant rent and company store prices. When the coal boom in Clay died out in the 1950s, closing down many of the smaller mines and diminishing the influence of the large companies, the miner still had his little patch of land where he could grow a little to tide him by. So the problem left by mechanization, was, in Kentucky, a crisis of no jobs, not as in Mississippi, a tragedy of no jobs, no homes, no lands, and no gardens.

Without a job, a man in the mountains must either get by on what little he can raise on his acre or two of level ground and what he can buy with food stamps, or he must leave the mountains for the cities. The men who are crippled by injury or too enfeebled to work must try to cope with a welfare system that is destructive in all aspects, terribly inefficient, and frustratingly hostile. If a man had never owned a house and farm out of town, but instead had been born into one of the semi-rural, semi-urban, slum hollers near town where he had no room for a garden, then he would be totally at the mercy of the welfare department—left destitute by its denial of benefits or left forever in debt because the check would not make ends meet.

In itself, there may not be too much wrong with living in an old, half-sound house up a dirt back road if the man can make sixty dollars a week at a garage, and the woman has an acre of land on which to tend vegetables—though most families in such situations might wish there were more chances to do better. But most people are not that well off. Either the acre of land is missing, or the sixty dollars a week is missing or substituted for by thirty-five dollars welfare, or both land and income are missing. There are many families, lacking everything but irregularly available food stamps, who live in conditions no better than does the displaced tenant farmer in Mississippi. In general, however, the coal mining generations survived their working years with a little more, mainly in terms of land, than did the cotton farming generations of Mississippi—though in both places there are left no jobs, few young people, and hard times. It is difficult, though, to calculate the loss to Kentucky of its mountain resources, which truly seemed to give little but misery to the people who inherited the rich mountain lands from their forefathers of one hundred and fifty years ago.

Poor people view their plight from much different perspectives in the Delta and in the mountains. The history of the black man in the Delta is one of slavery, racial oppression, economic exploitation, violent suppression, and political disfranchisement. He accurately sees the roots of his present troubles in the white planter's and businessman's unconcern for himself as a black working man and in the lack of power he himself holds in the politics and economics of his community. He sees no help coming to him from the federal government which manifests itself in the Delta in the form of welfare departments, employment programs encouraging him to leave the state or requiring him to take a job that no white man would be given, and in the Head Start programs, most of which were at one time or another defunded by OEO. He directs his struggles largely through independent groups such as the NAACP and the Freedom Democratic Party whose battlefields have mainly been street demonstrations, economic boycotts of stores, and political campaigns for local office. Poor people, to him, means "black people," though he believes that small farming whites also have been victims of the "big man's" system; and he shows great unity of hopes and of purposes with his neighbors. Everyone has been treated alike, and everyone has understood that treatment from the cradle up. Though many have been immobilized or dispirited by years of revolving indebtedness and the family ties of the plantation, just as many have shown that they will still fight as people from the plantations in Humphreys County fought to build their Head Start. A movement for human dignity still continues, though sometimes underground, and is felt in Mississippi.

In Kentucky, most men agree that things are hard because there are no jobs. The man who does have a job or works in a mine knows he cannot make anything because, "the big man at the top takes it all." Past that point, people have had trouble isolating things that should be blamed for all their grievances. County officials and the welfare department are uniformly distrusted, and it is believed that these people do not encourage, and probably hinder, factories coming into the area. It is hard for people to log blame against the rich man, for outside of the big mine operators and truck fleet owners who are considered to be exploiters, there are not many rich people in the mountains. A kind of formless hostility is felt for the "big man," the man seen as a directing force on county and state politics, who lives comfortably, who owns a lot of property scattered around a county, who can hand out jobs on the highway department or the county, who puts money into elections and tries to coerce the poor people to vote a certain way. But there are too many "little men" or poor men who try to achieve these same things, or who pass money for or fraternize with the powerful men; this sort of corrupt, oppressive maneuvering reaches so far down into poor communities and is so much a part of mountain life that little is done to fight it.

Southeastern Kentucky miners were once united in their struggle for higher wages, better conditions, and a union, but there has been since that time no other movement in poor mountain communities to compare with the movement that has been seen in Mississippi and the South.

There have been, however, many counties where people have united for the purpose of achieving specific goals. During the 1960s, statewide movements addressed to specific problems have been seen: in the West Virginia miners' strike for black lung legislation, and in the anti-strip mine campaign, active primarily in Kentucky. Most of these efforts have been extremely militant, and if they have not all been successful in the sense of winning their causes, they have succeeded in the sense that people decided for themselves what needed to be done and tried hard to do it. Most of them, for that matter, have been more effective in achieving their goals than have the programs directed by outsiders, and virtually all have been more important, in terms of people learning that they too have the right to speak out, than anything that the government has offered (except possibly the first rare moments of the War on Poverty when mountain men felt that the project might be important enough to fight for and remove from the hands of local politics).

But the mountain poor have not been confronted with such an obvious array of hostile forces as have the black poor in Mississippi, nor have they been able, across the region, to unite as poor people. Faults in the American economic system, callousness toward land, labor, people, and the future lies behind most of what has beset the mountains today. In Mississippi, the problem lies less with the inhumanity of an economic structure than with the inhumanity born of racial oppression. It is hard, in Kentucky, to strike out at the economic system because, in large measure, it does not function there. There is no big business; there are no factories to treat men unjustly, and it is hard to perceive who might be responsible or before whom grievances ought to be laid. So, lesser enemies have been selected —the highway department that builds no roads, the welfare department that operates unfairly, and county and school officials who provide nothing to ease the burden of poverty. Yet people have rarely rallied against these bodies because while they do little for the poor, they control more non-farm jobs in a given county than any single industry, and because they can wield great power against any individual family or community that struggles against them. For the most part, then, when poor people have joined together to do things over the last few years, their interest has been mainly to make use of programs, primarily OEO—to right some of the conspicuous aspects of poverty, inadequate pre-school care, bad housing, inadequate food, illiteracy, and insufficient clothing. Whether these are to be the sum of a nation's efforts to repair a region spanning the eastern seaboard and to repay the debt of extracted coal remains a question.

COMPARISON TO THE SITUATION OF SOUTHERN WHITES

The Appalachians run deep into Georgia and Alabama, cover one-third of Tennessee, much of North Carolina and Virginia, and a corner of South Carolina. In the mountain parts of these states the men like to consider themselves rednecks about as much as hillbillies, and this is also the case for a goodly number of Kentuckians. It is perhaps valuable to draw some distinctions between the attitudes of poor white Kentucky hillbillies and poor white southern rednecks. It would not be correct to identify Kentucky with the South, for while cars may sport Confederate-flag license tags, and while Atlanta has attracted many young men from the hills, eastern Kentucky as a whole thinks of itself as more allied with states like West Virginia, and has come more under the influence of Ohio, Indiana, and Michigan than of the industrial South.

White southerners, in farming areas, feel themselves to be in league with the large planters, businessmen, and politicians who run their county and state. They are used to the system where the prosperous and powerful, who must rely for their support on somebody, look out for what they believe to be the interests of the poor white, in terms of jobs, welfare, debt paying, and other matters. Their own situation, as they see it, is that if they are to make a living on a small farm, they must have the help of the successful farmers and businessmen; and if they are to make a living at a factory job, they must not be made to compete with a greater number of poor blacks who also need work. They fear the black man getting their jobs more than they dislike the rich whites for excluding them from political and economic decisions. So, in areas like the Mississippi Delta, where whites seldom openly contest each other in local politics and where there is a central authority—the planter— the poor whites abide by the decisions that reach them and do as they are bid. But in the larger areas of the South, less dominated by traditional powers and where the status quo cannot be so smoothly maintained, the poor whites can become as bitterly frustrated in their needs as can poor men in Kentucky or poor black men in the South. Often enough they will turn to the Klan for a way out, but the Klan just tells them that the poor whites are in a fight every step of the way with the black men who wants the same things, and the black men have got the government behind them. And it is quite true that agencies like OEO have succeeded, in the South, in serving mainly the black poor (or the white politicians and civic leaders who have assumed control of the programs).

In the mountains of Kentucky, relations between poor whites and poor blacks are very confused. In most counties blacks number only three or four per cent of the population, and that is almost entirely concentrated around the county seats. Some counties, like Harlan, have large black communities, for men came up out of the coal fields of Alabama and Tennessee to work the mines of Kentucky. Where whites and blacks have worked together, there is virtually no animosity between the groups, and indeed, it is likely that before the dual ascendancy of the civil rights movement and television in the late 50s and early 60s, most Kentucky whites knew little of the racial situation in other areas. Mountain people have always figured that everybody is different in one way or another, and that there is not much you can do about it. In Clay County, whites do not really think one way or another about the black community in Manchester; it has never been a cause of concern for them. All area-wide poor people's groups join together, whites and blacks, and the fiercest speakers in the Cumberland Valley are black ministers and miners. Adjoining Clay County is Jackson County, and there no black family has ever been allowed to settle down. It is the only Kentucky mountain county of which that is true, and it is a rather inexplicable phenomenon. Of course the news from the cities on TV has disturbed some whites, but a lot of poor whites have remarked, "What we need down here is one of those black power people. Then we'd get organized."

It should be stressed that the poor white in the South is caught between those two identifications: poor and white. To too many, the "southern white" represents the ruling class of the South, and therefore also the poor. And it is the particular problem of the poor white that he has too long relied on his affluent neighbor to see him through times of trouble. Now he is in the rather helpless position of seeing black men around him pulling themselves up faster than he can, and the only lasting organization open to poor whites in the South, the Klan, has been unable to come up with a solution to his problems yet.

The Deep South is very unlike the mountain areas such as eastern Kentucky in that it views itself much as a rival civilization to the rest of America. Southern values, especially those built upon race and religion, have been spurned by the North. The divide between the Protestant fundamentalism of Georgia and the libertinism of New York that is portrayed on southern TV and radio is really enormous. Mountain people in Kentucky share some of these attitudes about northern cities, but they are manifested as dismay and wonder that such things could go on, whereas many white southerners think of their region as a last entrenchment against heathen free thinking. Young people in the rural South differ little from their parents on these issues, but in the mountains young people are very casual about city influences, and some wear long hair and sport mustaches and listen to the rock music broadcast from Lexington and Cincinnati.

Southern whites are extremely concerned about halting communism, and they consider themselves, in that respect, very patriotic. The Vietnam war is much supported in the South, though little faith is put in Washington's ability to handle it. Mountain people, too, consider themselves patriotic, but rarely involve themselves with issues like "communism." They are willing to go to war if everybody else is going because they do not believe themselves any better than other people. Most mountain communities were left almost bereft of men during the Second World War. Thousands of men left for the war plants in Detroit and Oak Ridge, and thousands more dug coal at the big mines which were kept open during the war. Barely a family did not lose a relative in combat. Those years left the mountain people with little enthusiasm for wars, and the war in Vietnam has been widely hated as being for no good purpose. It is part of an ingrained distrust for elected men that mountain people do not really accept the excuses for fighting there that this country has offered. Neither are they comfortable at having sons so far from home.

Conclusion

One of the most remarkable things about the 1960s was that people who were not themselves poor or as a group actually oppressed did show their willingness to become involved in America's social movements toward economic and political justice. But the problems of this nation's poor people have shown themselves to be not so simple that those unfamiliar with each group's specific wants could lead the struggle. It is difficult enough to suggest massive solutions to the poverty of the Mississippi Delta or the Kentucky mountains without searching for solutions that will fit throughout the South, the Appalachians, or the country.

Though their thinking is often ignored by professional poverty fighters, poor people themselves have desires for and about change. These desires are often not well articulated, but sometimes they are quite clear. The black movement throughout the South, the store boycotts in Mississippi, the development of Head Start centers through organizations like the Child Development Group of Mississippi and Friends of the Children of Mississippi, the fight against strip mining on mountain land waged in Kentucky, Tennessee, and West Virginia—all have been efforts poor people carried through for definite ends. These were not movements where the outsider conceived the problem and rallied the poor around him to support the cause. They were all expressions of anger and of hope that sprang directly from the needs and frustrations of people who have been kept down and left to waste away.

If it is not his wish to abort or to redirect the desperate want for change in poor communities, the concerned outsider can play a definite role by helping poor people to come together so that they may better express the changes that they seek. Too often, that role is overstepped and the outsider gives in to the temptation to lead the people who all of their lives have been led this way and that, and always been denied the chance to run things themselves.

What the outsider, be he a representative of a government agency, church group, or a private agency, may well not understand is that his solution to poverty, which usually involves the creation of "opportunities" for individual improvement, though excellent in itself, does not address itself to the main problem. The essential responsibility is not the poor man's to try to adapt himself to "opportunities" which, in fact, are not generally provided by the solutions of the outsider; rather it is the responsibility of the nation, as represented by government and business, to pay off the debt owed men and women who, after well-serving the builders of the twentieth century, have found that they have had taken from them virtually all the things which were important to them and all the things which made them important in the eyes of the world. Whatever the form of the repayment, it must be more substantial than increased "opportunities." It might be enough if the debt were admitted and the process halted—the process by which people are used and then discarded for the sake of the production and progress.

The need is for social change. It is fruitless to expect that this will be spawned from within the social, economic, or political structure, from within the system, for laws and institutions are by their nature inflexible; they do not foster change but, at best, yield to change after it has begun to occur. Social change comes from people, people for whom change is a necessity—the industrial worker during the first decades of this century, the southern black during the 1960s. We make the mistake when looking for solutions to poverty of thinking in terms of huge efforts, dramatic legislation, mammoth inventions like OEO. This creating of new institutions does little to encourage the energetic development of society. It is a dead-end process, both when the institution is manufactured by the government, as was OEO, and when it is a product of a social movement, as are the modern trade unions. For many working men, their union is a problem just like their employer. For many poor people, OEO is a problem along with the forces they feel are oppressing them.

America's problems are many, and they are not so simple that they can be solved through handouts to the poor or by giving jobs to the unemployed as a means of elevating them. This is no longer a country in which it is a pleasure to work, to physically build. It is no longer a country in which the good life can go untainted. As a nation, we have lost our spiritual footing. We have built too much too fast, created and became enmeshed in too large a structure, a bureau-structure that is programmed only for "progress," and we no longer have an understanding of what we have done, are doing, or what we want.

We have developed two terrible traits. We feel unable to stand up and air our own beliefs and grievances because— in a society that is not highly integrated but enormously complex and virtually incomprehensible—we have lost the sense of our own self-importance. And we have developed a conservatism within us that is suspicious of, and that causes us to obstruct, the outcries of those who have found it within themselves to stand up. We have come to believe that our problems can best be solved through institutional leadership. We resent those who deny this.

America needs new voices. We need to cherish each new voice and to cherish our own. We need, for the benefit of each of us, not to encourage the extension of what has become the American way of life to the millions who now exist apart from the system—the black, the poor white, etc. —for they will not, as cultural identities, fit into the system but will be crushed by it, leaving it unchanged; rather, we need to encourage their separate development, encourage their willingness to challenge the system, so that perhaps they will reinvigorate us all, make us remember that we too have a right to be dissatisfied and that we too have a right to seek satisfaction.

When we look around us at what has become an uncomfortable society and realize the horrible fact that it has coughed up some twenty to forty million souls for whom it has decided that there is no further use, let us not be hasty to play more games with those men's lives by redirecting our institutions toward their material improvement but instead encourage them to fight back so that we might know how such a fight is waged.

This book proposes no solutions to the problems of poor people or of poverty as a national fault, except that of calling upon the reader to support or at least stand out of the way of men who, from a sense of anger, of need, and of social justice, have come to represent by many methods, and to many ends, their interests as they perceive them.

It might be better if, as you read this, another document about the pain and unfairness of poverty in America, you did not first wonder what could be done to help these people but instead wonder how it happened that a society which, in founding, paid more than lip service to the idea of free men, became emptied of joy and unconscious of the worth of men, and look for a means of personal, not just national, salvation.

Postscript

During the time that has gone by since *Our Land Too* was finished, some important things have happened in Louise and in the mountains.

The schools of Yazoo City complied with federal order and peacefully desegregated during the 1969–70 year. The children of many of Louise's white families had been going to these schools since the white school of Louise was shut down to avoid desegregating. Most of these children have now begun going to a private school in Silver City, Humphreys County.

In the spring of 1970, Rainey Pool, a one-armed, black plantation worker, was beaten and shot to death in Louise after an incident outside a "white" nightspot. The murder stunned both the white and the black communities, for in the Delta, land of the gentleman planter, public killings are not supposed to take place. The black community reacted by beginning a boycott of the town's businesses. It is the first concerted act of resistance seen in Louise, and it has brought out resentments which for years have been buried within people. When the Sunflower River was dragged for Rainey Pool's body, the bodies of two other black men were discovered. The parents of both young men had thought they were in Chicago.

Kentucky and West Virginia in the summer of 1970 have seen coal strikes which have kept up to twenty thousand men away from work. The work stoppage has been caused by picket lines manned by disabled union miners. The picketers have been demanding that their union grant them hospital benefits from the time they become disabled, rather than withholding them until the miner reaches retirement age. The men who are staying off their jobs complain that the Federal Mine Safety Act is not being enforced either by the government or by the union.

It was the feeling among the strikers that the president of the United Mine Workers, Tony Boyle, has not been sensitive to his men's demands. He has declared that the UMW welfare and retirement fund, one of the richest union treasuries in the country, cannot afford to increase benefits; and, on top of the increase he gave during his re-election campaign in 1969 and the fund's notorious ill-management, he may be right. He tells the men that if they want a more prosperous union, they should return to work, for on each ton of coal they mine, the company pays forty cents into the union's welfare fund.

One result of this confrontation between men and the union which has ceased to represent them is that coal production in the United States dropped 20 per cent. The operating mines of eastern Kentucky have been working extra shifts to capitalize on the national demand. A ton of coal now costs fifteen dollars in the mountains. They say that by the winter it will be twenty.

In June 1970, the fiscal court of Knott County, in a meeting attended by several hundred angry landowners, banned strip mining within the county limits. It is questionable under Kentucky law whether or not a county has that authority. The Reclamation Department apparently decided that Knott County did not, for it issued permits to several companies to begin stripping operations.

A controversy has begun to rage concerning the damage that coal trucks do to public roads. The trucks, weighing with their coal as much as fifty tons, carry licenses good only to half that amount and drive roads that often have a weight limit as low as ten tons. Both the battle against the strippers and the battle against the trucks have seen, during the course of this summer, armed citizens demanding relief from the law.

Clay County seems to be in for a new boom in coal. A great deep mine is about to open, promising to employ 150 men and operate throughout the decade. At the same time, four new stripping operations have begun. To leave the main highway and travel to what was only a few months ago near-virgin countryside is to see the ruin that a bulldozer, in just a week or two, can make of a rugged and wild green mountain.

—TONY DUNBAR

Goose Creek, Kentucky
August 13, 1970

Tony Dunbar grew up in Georgia and South Carolina. He has worked in community programs in rural Georgia and in Atlanta, where he spent two summers as a fieldworker for the Voter Education Project. He was with the Appalachian Volunteers for a year and with the Mountain Legal Rights Association one summer, working with welfare recipients and on strip mining. He is now an undergraduate student in Boston.